# TABLE OF CONTENTS

# BEYOND EXTREMISM, HATRED AND VIOLENCE
## Toward a More Peaceful World

R.E. Markham

# SHIRES✿PRESS

4869 Main Street
P.O. Box 2200
Manchester Center, VT 05255
www.northshire.com

BEYOND EXTREMISM, HATRED
AND VIOLENCE
Toward a More Peaceful World
©2017 by R.E. Markham

ISBN: 978-1-60571-376-2

*Building Community, One Book at a Time*
*A family-owned, independent bookstore in*
*Manchester Ctr., VT, since 1976 and Saratoga Springs, NY*
*since 2013. We are committed to excellence in bookselling.*
*The Northshire Bookstore's mission is to serve as a resource for*
*information, ideas, and entertainment while honoring the needs*
*of customers, staff, and community.*

*Printed in the United States of America*

# DEDICATION

To all those who wish to enjoy a vital existence
without fear of violence.

# ACKNOWLEDGMENTS

Janet Keep was a valued mentor and advisor, meeting with me many times and encouraging my efforts when I was writing an earlier version of my book. Thanks to Henry Thomas who, after questioning my approach to another draft, said "Just say what you believe!" Sandra Cantwell's enthusiastic comments came at a time when I had begun to have doubts about my ideas. Deborah Edson also offered valued support. My editor, Deborah Brown, improved my use of the English language and recommended some structural changes. My daughter, Amy Markham, read every essay with a critical and constructive eye and made many helpful suggestions. Debbi Wraga patiently and professionally made sure formatting decisions maintained consistency. Jon Pritchard has been very helpful with marketing suggestions and Mary Garnish contributed her design expertise. I'm also thankful for fruitful discussions with Philip Eddy, the Reverends Robert Buckwalter and Mark Longhurst, and comments made by many friends and relatives, among them being Carolyn Behr, Dick and Jeanne Blake, Steve Bolinger, Peggy Coverdale, Stuart Crampton, Joe Manning, Darrel Murray, Robert Pennock and his fellow pastors, Jean Robinson, Brian Voogh, the Reverend Donna Schaper, and my sisters Elinor Myers and Mary Coverdale.

When doubts surface, what would writers do without the support of others?

# PREFACE

I was eleven years old, alone under a tree on a hot Kansas afternoon, when I found myself asking: "Why am I here?" "Why do any of my surroundings exist?" "Why is the earth here, the sun, the stars, even the universe?" "Why is there anything at all?" "If God is the reason for all of existence, why is there God?" Of course, I had no answers. I awoke out of my reverie, and as I returned to daily life, everything felt strange, as though I were in a dream.

My normal activities soon covered over my questions and the mysterious nature of my experience. I resumed living in the reality with which I was familiar. But whenever I recall my first awareness of mystery, I again have the feeling that existence is an enigma and that our vast accumulation of knowledge doesn't come close to capturing the whole of reality.

Why is it so difficult to accept that what we conventionally think of as reality is a fraction of the whole? Although the deep level of reality is eternally present, we usually aren't immediately aware of that dimension because we are immersed in the challenges and the topsy-turvy of daily existence, and because we are predominantly conditioned to customary ways of seeing, interpreting, and making sense of the world. This is true no matter who we are - rich, poor, black, white, Christian, Muslim, Russian, American, intellectual or anti-intellectual, fundamentalist, secularist, homeless, a criminal, a law-abiding citizen, or some other identity.

Our many and varying points of view make up a rich and evolving tapestry of human existence, but our thinking and our ways of behaving often obscure what underlies existence and the mystery of why anything exists at all. We are blitzed by what lies on the surface - by advertisements urging us to need what we want instead of wanting what we need, by the stream of

1

messages from more and more avenues of communication, by slogans, by religious and political promises, by lies or fake news, and much more. It is easy to allow ourselves to be swept along with whatever wind is blowing. With so much talk and cacophony, for and against, from the left and the right, individuals and groups are more and more easily caught up taking combative sides of you're wrong/I'm right. The end results too often lead to extremism, hatred and violence and to forgetting and/or ignoring the deep dimension underlying all of what exists. It's enough to make one want to say "Stop the world; I want to get off."

The craziness will not be diminished by a new political or religious ideology consisting of elaborate beliefs and rituals. Neither side of the culture war will win out over the other. We need a radical perspective that acknowledges a fathomless and wordless dimension of reality, the awareness of which throws our human meanderings and struggles into relief.

The essays in Part One argue for the constant presence of this dimension in our lives even when we are unaware of it. To show how this dimension can undermine extremism, hatred, and violence, Part Two contrasts conventional and radical perspectives on what it means to be an individual, on how we think of community, and on how we interpret power, love, and compassion. Because religions have played positive and negative roles in helping us try to achieve a more peaceful world, Part Three compares religion and spirituality and offers different interpretations of Christianity including one undercutting tendencies toward extremism, hatred, and violence. Part Four highlights the significance of an ancient theme, asks "Where Do We Go From Here?" and adds a personal note. Appendix A offers some recommendations for how individuals and groups might act to minimize the madness of living only in a limited reality.

2

# PART ONE
# A RADICAL PERSPECTIVE[1]

I suspect the notion of an inexplicable dimension of depth underlying all of existence might be strange to many people. The essays in Part One argue that a deep level of reality is not improbable or far-fetched. I elaborate on what I mean by "reality," "existence," and "worlds," point out the fallibility of human existence, highlight how our ability to use language and other symbols can lead us to be unaware of deep reality and to forget that we are part of nature. I argue that adopting a radical perspective can enhance opportunities to minimize the extremism, hatred and violence so prevalent today.

---

[1] When I use the adjective "radical," I don't consider it synonymous with "extremism." The latter applies to absolute positions held by individuals and groups within conventional reality; "radical" refers to the depth dimension underlying all of existence. It's possible to have a radical perspective and have extreme viewpoints, but being an extremist is not compatible with having a radical perspective. Accepting a radical perspective undermines extremism.

3

# REALITIES, EXISTENCE, WORLDS

What if daily experiences do not constitute the only reality? Must we not acknowledge the possibility that there may be two levels of reality, one consisting of our conventional views of what is real and the other being a deeper dimension about which we can be aware but which is inaccessible to our senses and intellect? If reality is to be all encompassing, must it not refer both to what we humans can experience **and** to unknowns beyond? Perhaps this deeper dimension is vastly greater than what we normally experience. Perhaps it is the ultimate source out of which all existence emanates. Perhaps it is the mysterious context within which we live our lives and which reveals the limitations of conventional realities.

<u>Two Realities</u>

Conventional reality includes everything in existence: Mountains, clouds, rivers, pebbles, dirt, the sun, stars, galaxies, every animal and plant, bacteria, atoms and molecules, sounds, sights, thoughts, ideas, opinions, prejudices, ideologies, religions, other people, everything we can actually or potentially experience. It includes every event and happening: wars, love affairs, disagreements, diverse cultures, plans, strategies, schemes, habits, rituals, extremist points of view, hatred, violence, everything we conventionally consider to be real, every daily situation, everything reported in the news, everything shared on social media, everything under the sun and in the universe, and all of our feelings about these existents.

Beneath all existing things, events, and feelings is a deeper level of reality, far vaster that what we normally experience. Eckhart Tolle metaphorically refers to this deeper level as the ocean beneath all the ripples on the surface. This deep reality cannot be defined. It's a vast mystery. It is eternally present but defies comprehension. It is beyond human ken and cannot be analyzed. It's invisible, a kind of potent abyss which can be pointed to but not seen. It is eternal, beyond our three-dimensional ways of seeing, beyond our limited categories of space and time. It's the ultimate source of all existence out of which everything emanates. It undercuts hatred and violence and supports people coming together in times of crisis regardless of their existential differences.

The two realities are not separate; there's an interpenetration of the two levels. The deeper level is the unconditioned source of freedom, creativity, courage, love, and potency even though we may think these qualities originate with us and are our possessions. It's not easy consciously to fuse the dimensions in one's day-to-day experience, to recognize that everything one can see and touch and hear also has a deeper dimension. For example, more often than not, I am completely out of touch with a deeper dimension and look out upon others and upon other things as objects. And, indeed, without the awareness of that deeper dimension, they **do** become objects in **my** environment, objects in **my** egocentric world. They are what I construct them to be, and I relate to them based upon those constructions. It is only when I am in touch with a deeper dimension that I can appreciate the depth of other people and beings in my environment and thereby experience communion with them. Often, it's difficult to do although it is basically simple. We don't want to give up our constructions because we are comfortable with them and they seem to provide some stability in the midst of changing circumstances.

## Existence

Existence is synonymous with everything described as constituting the conventional level of reality. Every existent form shares the following characteristics: Uniqueness, Change, Interaction, History, and Depth.

Uniqueness.--Every mountain is different from every other mountain, no two rivers are the same, suns are unique in at least some ways as are galaxies. Species of animals and plants share similarities, but each individual animal and plant is at least somewhat different. Every sound and sight is unique as is each thought, ideology, and emotion. Every person is unique, even twins. Families differ as do all groups and countries. Every existent form is unique.

Change.--Our universe is changing and evolving toward an unknown future. Everything which seems so solid will someday be no more. My desk, my computer, the rug in my room, my dwelling place, roads, cars, factories, skyscrapers , all buildings and other human constructions which seem to provide some stability in our worlds are undergoing minute, incremental changes and someday will disappear. That's hard to accept, but not if we consider all of existence from the perspective of hundreds, thousands, millions, or billions of years.

Interaction.--Every existing thing interacts with others. Nothing exists in a vacuum. Every existent is in some relationship with others and would not "be" otherwise. Nothing would survive without being connected in numerous ways with other elements of changing circumstances and environments. Our very identities are formed and conditioned by our natural and social environment and are altered as we engage with others.

History.--Pick up a pencil. It has a history. Every object has a history. Every process or ritual has a history. All our thoughts, religions, ideologies, have histories. All plants and animals (including humans) have a history. They never were just as they are now and they will never be just so again. Every existent in the universe has a history as does the universe itself which is not a static thing but a process.

Depth.--Focus intently on any object. Imagine what is beneath its surface appearance. It has constituent parts and each of those parts is unique, changing, interacting, and has a history. But where do they all come from? We could analyze *ad infinitum* and not arrive at their ultimate origins. We must learn to accept that all of existence is a manifestation of a depth dimension we can never define or pin down no matter how much we employ our cognitive abilities. It's truly a vast mystery that anything exists at all.

## Worlds

The longer I live, the more I've come to a fuller appreciation of the tremendous richness and variability of all forms of life. All are in continual flux, some forms changing more rapidly than others. There are as many worlds as there are sentient beings and each world is different from others in at least some way. In his book, *An Essay on Man,* Ernst Cassirer interprets the biologist Jakob von Uexkull as saying:

> Reality is not a unique and homogeneous thing; it is IMMENSELY diversified, having as many different schemes and patterns as there are different organisms. Every organism is, so to speak, a monadic being. It has a world of its own because it has an experience of its

own. The phenomena that we find in the life of a certain biological species are not transferable to any other species. The experiences--and therefore the realities--of two different organisms are incommensurable with one another. In the world of a fly, says Uexkull, we find only `fly things'; in the world of a sea urchin we find only `sea urchin things.' (p.23)

Cassirer suggests we might use this framework for understanding the diversities of human worlds:

> Is it possible to make use of the scheme proposed by Uexkull for a description and characterization of the human world? Obviously this world forms no exception to those biological rules which govern the life of all the other organisms. Yet in the human world we find a new characteristic which appears to be the distinctive mark of human life. The functional circle of man is not only quantitatively enlarged; it has also undergone a qualitative change. Man has, as it were, discovered a new method of adapting himself to his environment. Between the receptor system and the effector system, which are to be found in all animal species, we find in man a third link which we may describe as the symbolic system. This new acquisition transforms the whole of human life. As compared with the other animals man lives not merely in a broader reality; he lives, so to speak, in a new dimension of reality. (p. 24)

Worlds in nature overlap sufficiently to form species; when individual human worlds overlap, they form groups ranging from those which are informal to those as extensive as a culture. Every situation involves worlds which can either be

9

compatible with one another, **or** in conflict as when animals compete for food and resources and as when human worlds clash because they seem to threaten one another. So far as we know, animals cannot transcend their biological and instinctual differences, but it's possible for humans to avoid being trapped in their egoistic differences by being open to the depth underlying all existence.

To summarize, trillions of life forms, each having its particular world view, constitute existence and what we normally think of as reality. But this conventional level of reality is but a fraction of all that is real and tends to obscure awareness of a far vaster level of reality that is beyond our capability to describe or analyze.

2

# THE FALLIBILITY OF BEING HUMAN

To recognize human fallibility is to accept that we live in a universe that is incomprehensibly vast and billions of years old. Astronomers tell us there are billions of stars in our galaxy and billions of galaxies of similar or greater size. They tell us the number of stars exceeds the grains of sand on all the beaches of the earth and that the nearest star is over four light years away, meaning it would take that many years traveling at 186,000 miles per second to come close to its vicinity. We may "know" these supposed facts, but normally we don't let their significance sink in because we are immersed in the daily challenges of our time and place.

Another way to recognize our fallibility is to accept we are only one of many species on this infinitesimally small speck of dust. Millions of species have come and gone. Humans have been around for a mere fraction of time in the history of the universe so why do we think we are immune to the forces of nature? Many species are in the process of disappearing and it remains an open question whether *homo sapiens* will survive, something which will depend largely on minimizing extremism, hatred, and violence and maximizing inclinations for love, compassion, and deep community. The future of our species hangs in the balance.

The centuries-long impressive accumulation of knowledge doesn't guarantee our survival. It deludes us into thinking our human accomplishments demonstrate we are a favored species having presumed superiority over all others. Such *hubris* overlooks the fact that there is so much we don't know. Think of the times we thought our decisions were sound, only to find out later they were short-sighted. There's a lot of truth to saying "We can never know where we are until after we've left there." It's only when we move past particular mind-sets that we see how limited and conditioned we were.

We may acknowledge that we don't know everything, but we think we know ourselves pretty well. For example, I know what ideas, opinions, and values make most sense to me, and I'm aware of memories and feelings about my personal past. But I can never know the full contents of my subconscious, let alone my share of the collective unconscious of our species. I don't fully understand how and why certain passions, attitudes, dreams, or fantasies influence my behavior. Out of the myriad elements of my being, I likely select those which reinforce my self-image and self-esteem. Doing so helps me maintain some stability in my world and avoid being at loose ends, but in the process I may be sacrificing fuller potential richness of my life.

When preoccupied with our individual worlds, with the assumptions, perceptions, expectations, and thoughts that represent reality as we see it, it's easy to miss and/or distort the depths of others. I think I know my wife quite well. I know her interests, talents, significant experiences in her life, her long-standing hurts, and how she likely will respond in particular situations. But undoubtedly, there is so much I don't know, and I'll never be able to plumb the depths of her total being even if that were my desire. The same may be said about close friends and relatives, let alone all others with whom I interact. Any person I meet on a street could tell hundreds of stories, but most remain unspoken. So many unknowns, if known, could drastically change my perceptions of others and lead to different ways of relating to them.

There's so much we don't know about our surroundings. While teaching history to high school students years ago, I came across a book that made me aware of how limited our perceptions are. I've long forgotten the title and author of the book, but one chapter described walking down a street and becoming aware of sensing only the surface features of what was there. The author suggested picking out one building and asking questions: "Whose idea was it to build in just this location?" "What were the inspirations for its design?" "Who were the workers who constructed it and what was going on in their lives on the day they laid particular bricks?" "How many people have occupied this building and what were their hopes and dreams?" Answers to these question are probably lost. The point is that when we experience any situation, we generally perceive the way things appear to be at the moment and miss the story behind their existence. There's much more to each moment than we can ever know, perceive, or imagine.

By extension, there are also many events throughout history that we may never know, many more than what historians think they know. Think of the billions of humans who have lived and died about which we know nothing. How did they live from day to day? What were their cares, their joys, their disappointments? What was daily life like for the underlings in cold, dark castles? Or for pioneers who left behind belongings and loved ones, knowing they might never see them again. Yes, we have artifacts, remains of works of art, musical compositions, letters, and the published writings of a relative few, but these are mere scraps compared to all the history that has been lived. They provide tantalizing clues to the past and are the grist for historians but the full sweep and depth of happenings are lost forever. They may always be a mystery.

Scientists expand our understanding of phenomena that once were mysteries, but their successes don't make them immune to uncertainties. Knowing more may never be enough. Consider the theory of evolution, that species emerge and evolve when random mutations are "selected" by the environment and passed on to subsequent generations. I accept the general validity of this theory and yet find myself wondering why and how particular features of different species actually evolved. For example, what were the minute, incremental steps leading to the tuft on a tufted titmouse, to the single horn of a rhinoceros, or a peacock's remarkable plumage? How does each incremental step, such as slightly longer head feathers, s bump on the nose, or a slightly colored feather have sufficient survival value to be passed on to offspring?

How did particular behaviors evolve that became part of a species' repertoire? For example, what individual spider first secreted a filament, and how many generations did it take for subsequent spiders to instinctively fashion intricate geometrical webs? We take for granted that cats cover their waste, but what cat in ancient times first took such care, and what was the survival value of that practice? Entomologists have elaborate descriptions of the intricate communication abilities of dancing bees, but what was the first instance of such behavior and why did it occur? We marvel at flocks of birds dipping and swerving as one, but what ancient bird first followed another? Given the overwhelming evidence in support of evolutionary theory, we can assume that scientists refer to the process of natural selection to explain such phenomena and yet I'm still mystified by the origin and occurrence of such instinctive habits.

Since the time of Copernicus, astronomers have been revealing features of the universe. Currently, they contend that all matter was once collapsed into a single point no larger than the tip of a pencil. How can this be? How can even a sizable boulder be so compressed, let alone a mountain, a mountain range, all the oceans, the earth, our solar system, our galaxy, and the universe, including all the dark matter astronomers say exist? How did we get from that "point" to where we are now? They argue that it all began with the Big Bang but there remains the question of WHY that happened. That's a total mystery. And then there is the biggest conundrum of all, namely, why ANYTHING exists.

Is it not reasonable to accept the possibility that reality has a dimension that is an impenetrable void inaccessible to sense and intellect? Even scientists speak of the possibility of parallel universes we cannot directly experience because we are so accustomed to functioning in a three-dimensional world. For centuries, spiritual teachers and theologians have acknowledged the ultimate mystery of all existence. It's what the ancient Chinese called the Tao. It's what the theologian Paul Tillich calls the ultimate ground of all being. It's what the spiritual teacher Eckhart Tolle metaphorically refers to as the ocean far deeper than our individual ripples on the surface. It's the eternal dimension transcending our categories of space and time. It's the ultimate source of all we experience, actually or potentially. Without this dimension, where does all of nature and human existence come from? If we say everything is just a re-shuffling of prior existential elements, where did those elements come from? We can speculate about answers to this question, but our answers are human speculations and we can't ever be sure they constitute the absolute truth.

In the swirl of day-to-day happenings and challenges experienced and interpreted from the vantage point of conditioned individual worlds, we may still find ourselves reluctant to acknowledge the presence of a mysterious hidden dimension because it seems outlandish and because to do so questions our conventional notions of reality. But ignoring a deeper dimension leaves us prisoners of our conditioned ways of seeing things and makes us vulnerable to expressions of hatred and violence by those who believe they are the only ones who have the truth with a capital T. Might it not be better to accept a depth dimension as being the hidden context within which we live our lives and that we will not move beyond hatred and violence toward a more peaceful world until awareness of that deeper dimension removes any justification for animosity toward others?

I'm a bit hesitant to refer to the depth dimension as "Spirit" or "God" because of their anthropocentric connotations, but will do so anyway. If we deny God or Spirit, are we not left vulnerable to being caught up in the whirlwind of multiple symbol systems? Most are impressive, but some contribute to our experiencing conflict and breed hatred and violence. Accepting the mystery of God allows us to see our limited outlooks in longer and deeper perspective and allows Spirit to infuse our lives, opening the way for creative ways of solving problems and expressing love and compassion.

# 3

## HUMAN EXISTENCE[2]

Human perspectives are limited, yet the fact we are able to express them largely distinguishes us from other living things. As far as we know, plants and animals are not consciously aware of their existence and don't reflect upon why they are here, let alone contemplate the possibility of a depth dimension. That's not to say we share little with the rest of the plant and animal world because we certainly share a lot.

At any given moment millions of species and trillions of individual members of groups function and survive. Each species interacts with its environment, has a history, and emanates from some mysterious deep source. The same is true for billions of human beings.

Humans also share with all living things an instinct for survival, sometimes experienced as a struggle and sometimes as a desire to band together with others. Martin A. Novak, professor of biology and mathematics at Harvard University illustrates:

> My work indicates that instead of opposing competition, cooperation has operated alongside from the get-go to share the evolution of life on earth, from the first cells to *Homo sapiens* Life is therefore not just a struggle for survival—it is also, one might say, a snuggle for survival. (*Scientific American Magazine,* July 2012, p. 36.)

---

[2]Human existence is a subset of all existence.

We humans are no exception for we sometimes compete with others to preserve our point of view and often collaborate with others to achieve that aim. What distinguishes us from other life forms is our ability to use symbols, broadly defined.[3]

We can imagine that before our earliest ancestors created the use of symbols, their interactions with each other and with nature were direct and immediate. They were immersed in the flow of existence. When humans began to express themselves using rudimentary symbols by drawing pictures on cave walls, emitting guttural sounds or warnings, or some other means of representing their experience, they introduced another dimension into their lives, making it possible for them to become less a prisoner of their natural environment. Their experience and drive for survival led them to use symbols to distinguish themselves as different from others and to join with those of like mind in order to increase the chances of survival.

For centuries, billions of humans have steadily increased the number and variety of symbols. The accumulated result is an immensely rich and dense layer of symbols that overlay our sensory experiences and absorb our attention. They largely constitute the contents of our individual and collective mindsets and make possible expressing ideas to ourselves and to others.

Immersed in our symbol systems, we experience what we consider to be reality through the screen of these symbols. As Ernst Cassirer put it:

> No longer in a merely physical universe, man lives in a symbolic universe. Language, myth, art, and religion are parts of this universe. They are the varied

---

[3] I consider that symbols include languages, drawings, paintings, music, sculpture, diagrams, mathematics and any other form of expression intended to represent some facet of experience.

threads which weave the symbolic net, the tangled web of human experience....No longer can man confront reality immediately; he cannot see it, as it were, face to face. Physical reality seems to recede in proportion as man's symbolic activity advances. Instead of dealing with the things themselves man is, in a sense, constantly conversing with himself. He has so enveloped himself in linguistic forms, in artistic images, in mythical symbols or religious rites that he cannot see or know anything except by the interposition of this artificial medium. His situation is the same in the theoretical as in the practical sphere. Even here man does not live in a world of hard facts, or according to his immediate needs and desires. He lives rather in the midst of imaginary emotions, in hopes and fears, in illusions and disillusions, in his fantasies and dreams. (*An Essay on Man*, p. 25)

Television, computers, cell phones, Ipods, Ipads, blogs, Facebook, Twitter, and many other forms of electronic communication unknown to Cassirer provide ever-increasing ways to expand the spread of symbols. I don't question whether these tools have value, but I wonder if they interfere with our connection to nature and with awareness of the depth dimension of others and all existence. How often do we go somewhere without seeing people using their hand-held devices to communicate instead of interacting face to face?

Preoccupation with our symbol-laden worlds contributes to our sense of being separate beings. Alan Watts in *The Way of Zen* states:

The power of thought enables us to construct symbols of things apart from the things themselves. This includes the ability to make a symbol, an idea of ourselves apart from ourselves. Because the idea is so much more comprehensible than the reality, the symbol so much more stable than the fact, we learn to identify ourselves with our idea of ourselves. Hence the subjective feeling of a 'self' which 'has' a mind, of an inwardly isolated subject to whom experiences involuntarily happen. (p. 120)

It's important to acknowledge the many positive benefits of our continuing ability to create and use symbols. Symbols make possible talking to ourselves and others and also to create paintings, sculpture, dance, literature, music, architecture, mathematical systems, hundreds of diverse languages, scientific discoveries, and many other forms of expression. Without symbols, there would be no thoughts, no science, no religions, no philosophical systems, no diverse cultures, no music, no literature. Creative use of symbols makes possible the richness of our lives.

But the ability to use symbols does not always have positive effects. Symbols and symbol systems can be confining and restricting. When considering thought patterns to be accurate representations of experience, isn't there a tendency to cling to them and to resist perspectives that differ from ours? Operating out of our mindsets, don't we tune in to evidence that reinforces them and often dismiss or ignore ideas that question them? If, and when, we close ourselves off from experiencing more fully the facets of existence around us, we're more susceptible to becoming defensive, suspicious, less inclined to experience empathy, compassion, love, joy, and a feeling of deep community with others. The more our outlooks become rigid and dogmatic, the more we are inclined to be intolerant, to want to have control and power over those we perceive to be wrong-headed even to the point of expressing hatred toward them and threatening or doing violence. When we are convinced our individual symbolic worlds accurately represent the way things are, we aren't even aware of their limitations unless we are jarred out of them by some personal tragedy or catastrophic event that shocks us into recognizing our fallibility, finitude, and temporality.

Preoccupied and flooded daily with diverse symbol systems that are accentuated by the multiple means of expressing them, is it any wonder that we often feel bewildered by the resulting chaos and seek respite by retreating into and defending our individual and collective points of view? Is it possible our species has gone wild adding symbol systems which would be fine were it not for being mesmerized by their positive and negative effects? The culminating result is that we live in a kind of maelstrom of human creations generating swirling emotions, some of which lead to strife and conflict among those seeking to preserve their points of view.

More and more people recognize that we need to get some perspective on the madness of current human behavior lest we be overwhelmed to the point that existence of our species is in jeopardy. Gaining access to a deeper dimension which transcends the density of all existence is desirable. Practicing one form or another of meditation is one means. The key is to suspend our mind activity sufficiently to become aware of a deeper presence. By whatever means, humans have the ability to become aware of the mysterious depth that is the ultimate source of all that is, thereby increasing our ability to see the fallibility of rigid points of view and to live in ways that are more potent, creative, and compassionate.

# 4

# A RADICAL PERSPECTIVE

Adopting a radical perspective asks us to acknowledge we live in a universe that is incomprehensibly vast and that our species is recent among millions of others whose future like ours is in doubt.  A radical perspective recognizes that individuals are unique, constantly changing, and seek to preserve their mental outlooks when interacting with others. A radical perspective acknowledges and appreciates the many and diverse symbol systems which constitute human existence without assuming they represent all there is to know.  By accepting the eternal presence of an invisible dimension of reality individuals are able to recognize the many ways humans have sought to make meaning in their lives without insisting that any one way is necessarily better than any other.

Awareness of this depth dimension negates any person's claim to have absolute truth and undermines any dogmatically held set of convictions.  Even scientists tolerate the possibility that their carefully constructed and tested paradigms are not mirror reflections of some final and absolute reality.  They know theories are always subject to further verification.  Atheists may have good reasons to question the certainty of others' convictions, but consistency requires that "they too" apply the same skepticism to their own claims.  The bottom line is that it is presumptuous and preposterous for any person to claim possession of absolute truth and use that conviction to justify having animosity toward others who see things differently.

The same applies to formal groups.  True believers in any religion are not justified in thinking their beliefs are inviolable and that God is on their side.   No political party on the left or on the right has an exclusive corner on truth.  No corporate structure is so perfect that it merits monopolizing others. No country can legitimately claim its laws and values are absolutely superior to all others. All groups, formal and otherwise, have patterns of behavior, beliefs, and values made possible by the human ability to use symbols, but all of us need to accept that our existing symbol systems are constantly changing, have a history, interact with others, and, most of all, have their ultimate origins in a dimension underlying all existence.

Given the limitations of any world view and the recognition of human finitude, the adoption of a posture of humility seems a reasonable course for both individuals and groups to follow. But does this mean that belief systems, perceptions, conceptions, assumptions are all of equal value? For example, is the world view of those threatening others or using violence just as valid as any? Does acknowledgment of ultimate mystery necessarily lead to the chaos of indiscriminate relativism?

No, it doesn't. While we have good reason to question moral absolutes purporting to tell us what we should believe and how to act, we also don't need to accept the kind of relativism where any set of ideas is deemed just as good as any other. Just because we question the absolute truth of moral principles and guidelines doesn't mean they have no validity.

Those having a secular perspective have placed great stock in rational modes of inquiry as the method for avoiding extreme relativism and for constructing tentative truths. They recognize that, too often, impulse or habit rather than intelligence is used to arrive at solutions to challenging circumstances. But the exercise of reason can be overly analytical and blindly disregard awareness of a spiritual dimension. Reasoned solutions make judgments about right and wrong, good and bad, better or worse, and these judgments

24

imply something deeper at work even though it often is not clear what it is.

Neither belief in moral absolutes nor trust in rational modes of inquiry can legitimately claim to be the only way to avoid the chaos of indiscriminate relativism. Both avenues are human conventions and exist as manifestations of ultimate mystery. There is a role for faith in human lives, not blind faith in one or another religious tradition or faith in the supposed superiority of reason, but faith that there is a mysterious source being manifest throughout the evolving universe and perhaps other universes as well. If, and when, we suspend total allegiance to any symbol system, we can tap into the dimension of spirit and gain a deeper perspective which opens the way for thinking, feeling, and acting more compassionately and creatively instead of resorting to hatred and violence. Being open to spirit doesn't provide direct messages from an omnipotent God telling us what is right or wrong, but letting go of total commitment to particular world views opens the way for individuals to experience the strength and courage necessary to help withstand shallow impulses and cultural pressures.

Some will find this perspective difficult to accept. For example, fundamentalists may find it intolerable to give up the conviction that there are absolute truths and definite principles provided by God. Those of a secular bent of mind will find the notion of spiritual mystery too vague and will question how calling on an alleged deeper dimension is any help when having to resolve a difficult situation. So be it. I believe if we pause long enough to be open to the mysterious spirit within all of existence, we'll be less inclined to hate others or to threaten and employ violence. I do not suggest that we give up different and diverging points of view, but to develop ways to peacefully argue or disagree.

# PART TWO

# UNDERMINING EXTREMISM HATRED AND VIOLENCE

Suppose we accept that conventional views of reality are partial and often overlook an unfathomable, deeper dimension. What difference would it make? It would not deny the existence of all our conventional experiences of reality. It would not change the content of ideologies and religions or the positions taken by those on the left and the right side of the culture war. But it would help us recognize that all of our individual and collective world views are partial and the product of conditioning instead of being absolutely true. It would bring into play a deeper dimension to our normal ways of thinking that would change our attitudes toward the contents of our beliefs and perspectives.

To illustrate how awareness of a deep level of reality can make a difference, the following essays compare conventional and radical[4] interpretations of the individual, of community, and of power, love, and compassion. Conventional interpretations are compatible with extremism, hatred, and violence; radical interpretations undermine them and show how acceptance of a depth dimension can help contribute to a more peaceful world.

---

[4]Recall that "radical" refers to the depth dimension of reality. See footnote # 1 on page 3.

# INDIVIDUALISM AND INDIVIDUALITY

Today, we are witnessing the effects of what might be called the cult of the individual. Individualism says: "Do your own thing," "Establish your own identity," "Follow your bliss," "Just be yourself." These are a few of the messages defining the individual that arose after the conformity of the 1950s as described in C. Wright Mill's *White Collar*, Ayn Rand's *Atlas Shrugged*, and *The Lonely Crowd* by David Riesman, Nathan Glazer, and Reuel Denney. In the 1960s the influence of existentialism encouraged individuals to question the existence of moral absolutes and to choose their own values. More and more people decided to exercise their own freedom instead of being beholden to cultural norms and conventions or anyone else's choices and demands.

Within families, maxims such as "Spare the rod and spoil the child" and "Children are to be seen and not heard" were deemed old-fashioned. Today, children are lavished with gifts, told how special they are, encouraged to speak their minds and make choices once reserved for their parents. Marriages have fallen apart as partners pursued individual paths rather than make life-long commitments. There are exceptions, of course, but predominantly we're living in a fragmented society where many people value self-interest above community. Perhaps there are currently unknown positives to this trend but it alarms many who are accustomed to living in traditional forms of community.

We each have ideas, opinions, beliefs, feelings, and values that largely define ourselves as persons and distinguish ourselves from others. The fact that our viewpoints differ contributes to viewing ourselves as separate beings. When we emphasize our apparent separateness, we may not recognize that our views are largely the product of all the interactions evolved from our physical and cultural environments.

We are all conditioned persons. The more closely we identify ourselves with specific viewpoints, the more we form egos bent on survival either by cooperating with those who share our views and/or by competing with those who are different. Our behaviors become egocentric (egoic[5]) and we orient ourselves in the world as "me" instead of thinking in terms of "we"."

This tendency toward feeling as if we are separate identities had its origin thousands of years ago. Prior to the development of language, we can imagine the earliest members of our species did not have what we call self-awareness, did not "think" of themselves as separate from one another. Then, as they developed symbols they named themselves and features of their world and the earliest formation of rudimentary separate selves and egos began.

Thousands of generations later, our development as persons mirrors the evolution of our species. As newborn babies with spontaneous cries and random physical movements, we had little awareness of being separate entities. We were biological creatures with genetic characteristics inherited from our ancestors. From that early point, we were exposed to the cultural practices and values of our families and features of our surroundings. Gradually, random sounds and movements were reinforced by the human and physical environment, and became part of our behavioral repertoires. The critical axis was our acquisition of language. We internalized meanings associated with different sounds, learned names for things and events around us, and experienced others treating us as separate

---

[5]"Egoic" is a term used synonymously with egocentric by writers like Steve Taylor and Eckhart Tolle.

persons. By the time we were two years old or so, we were capable of moving around on our own, able to communicate with our loved ones, all of which contributed to our experience of having a distinct identity. Further development led to internalizing the norms and values of the culture, including the strong conviction that we are separate individuals. As Alan Watts observes in *Nature, Man, and Woman:*

> There is much to suggest that when human beings acquired the powers of conscious attention and rational thought they became so fascinated with these new tools that they forgot all else, like chickens hypnotized with their beaks to the chalk line. Our total sensitivity became identified with these partial functions so that we lost the ability to feel nature from the inside, and . . . to feel the seamless unity of ourselves and the world. (p.7)

Given the survival instinct we share with all species, we seek to preserve and perpetuate our identities. We tend to mingle with others who think as we do and derive a sense of security from these associations. Problems and challenges sometimes arise when we encounter others having different world views. Then, the possibility of conflict arises. We may defend our points of view or take issue with others. All of this is fine until we are so attached and identified with our ideas that we exhibit animosity toward others who differ, even to the point of experiencing hate, expressing threats and committing violence. Individualism leads us to relate to others as objects rather than to experience others in the fullness of their beings. Individualism can foster this dangerous result.

It doesn't have to be this way. Being human, we are conditioned by thoughts and emotions, but we needn't be "hung up" by them. Why not just "have them," like a possession? All possessions, even though they may be distinctive in some way, are not static. They've been picked up along the way of our journey and have a history. We may want to hold on to them because doing so gives us a sense of stability or permanence, but they are transitory, reliable only up to a point. As long as we overly attach ourselves to them they present roadblocks to peace; they are objects in our mind that interfere with full living. They constitute who we are as persons, as individuals, but don't take into account the wholeness of our being. From the vantage point of a deeper perspective, we can usually accept and appreciate that they define our individuality but we make a mistake by making our individual thoughts define all of who we are.

We can share our individuality in the world through the screens of our symbol systems, but the screens don't have to become walls over which we peer. They are boundaries between us and others, but they need not be impermeable. We can exhibit our characteristics, tell each other stories, enjoy the play of ideas, and express our opinions but without stumbling over conditioned rigid patterns of behavior.

There is nothing wrong with agreeing or disagreeing with others; that's what makes our existence interesting. But we need not come to blows, figuratively or literally. We need not hate others who differ. Others are making their way through life just as we are, and have a different take on things. Once we recognize they are essentially like us, we can give up any tendency to want control, thereby becoming more capable of empathy, love, and compassion.

When we realize that we are all deeply rooted in the ultimate source of life, we can better respect and acknowledge that we are all in this together. Being deeply rooted is the source of everyone's creativity, of freedom from conventions, and of novel expressions which make dialogue between us potentially joyful and fruitful. Let's enjoy our individuality instead of resorting to individualism. Individualism fosters conflict; individuality promotes peaceful relationships.

# 6

## CONVENTIONAL GROUPS AND DEEP COMMUNITY

We share with animate life forms the desire to associate with others of our species. Our ability to use symbols makes it possible to associate with our fellow humans not only because we share physical characteristics but also because we can communicate and be understood. Our associations or groups range from a few others as in friendships and families, to those of a much larger scale such as organizations and cultures. In between are numerous associations based on common interests, ethnic or racial identities, political preferences, religious beliefs, sexual orientation, cultural practices, just to name a few.

Whereas most associations are fluid and informal, conventional groups give structured expressions to particular ideas and practices. These can take the form of rules, guidelines, objectives, mission statements, job descriptions, organization charts, by-laws, rituals, constitutions, platforms, and many other forms expressed in symbols. Formal structures can facilitate smooth operations, provide stability to group members, and contribute to a sense of identity.

But just as conditioned beliefs and habitual patterns of individual behavior become so firmly established as to inhibit change and growth and foster defensiveness and even hatred of other persons, so can the structures of conventional groups become so rigid they potentially lead to violence. There are many examples of group members so obsessed with survival they cease to listen to alternative points of view. They hold onto their ways of thinking, become defensive, and see other individuals and groups as objects in their world or territory. Stereotyping and prejudices find fertile ground when members of groups are overly attached to their own perspectives. We all participate in groups, but challenges arise when group members identify themselves with group structures to the point they are absolutely sure their beliefs and practices are better than others. Just as individuality becomes reified as individualism, groups may erect figurative or even literal walls to keep out those who differ. Unrestrained individualism leads to egotism and narcissism; rigid group boundaries promote conditions that increase the potential for conflict.

Extreme individualism and exclusive groups undermine the possibility of moving toward a more peaceful world. Individuals and groups can move beyond narrow perspectives by accepting and becoming more aware of what underlies all of existence, a dimension that can help diminish the tensions among individuals and groups without requiring them to surrender their unique characteristics. Realizing that all perspectives are partial and fallible facilitates acknowledging the depth and particularity of others rather than perceiving them as objects in our world to be discriminated against or vilified.

I'm reminded of Martin Buber's distinction between what he calls "I-It" and I-Thou" relationships.

> For where there is a thing there is another thing. Every It is bounded by others. But when Thou is spoken, there is no thing. Thou has no bounds. (*I and Thou,* p.4)
>
> The relation to the Thou is direct. No system of ideas, no foreknowledge, and no fancy intervene between I and Thou. The memory itself is transformed, as it plunges out of its isolation into the unity of the whole. No aim, no lust, and no anticipation intervene between I and Thou. (*I and Thou*, pp. 11-12)

In *Slavery and Freedom* the passionate theologian Nikolai Berdyaev maintains that we largely live in the world of objectification in which all facets of our existence are treated as objects, including ourselves and others. These "objects" are the creation of our minds and we become captivated by them to the extent that we lose touch with the underlying realities they are intended to represent. We become slaves to objectification and sacrifice the freedom we could otherwise experience and express.

Temporarily suspending assumptions, conceptions, stereotypes and thoughts can help us realize that each of us is only one of many manifestations and configurations of energy within all of existence. When in a large gathering, instead of making quick judgments of others, categorizing them, stereotyping them, seeing them as objects, we can pause and remind ourselves that we all have rich histories and incalculable depths, that we are all particular events in an evolving universe. We can then lower our defenses, meet others more openly, and experience deep community with all living beings

I believe we may express our individuality **and** experience deep community with others whenever we accept and appreciate the spiritual dimension within, recognize our fallibility, release the hold of our preconceptions, and thus enjoy community with all who share with us the mystery of existence. This experience of deep community is manifest at any moment when we feel an essential oneness with others instead of just through any existing symbol-created screen. It is akin to the feelings people of different backgrounds have toward one another when they've endured a natural or social catastrophe together that has, at least temporarily, shaken their customary outlook and perceptions of others, and made their differences seem inconsequential. Feelings of deep community with others can't happen all the time; there's a place for habit, ritual and having different points of view. But it really takes very little effort to demonstrate to others that we respect their integrity, and thereby experience a sense of community with them without sacrificing our individuality.

7

# SOCIAL AND SPIRITUAL POWER

Individualism can lead to stressful relationships. Rigidly held group beliefs and practices can lead to extremism, hatred, and violence. Acceptance of a deep pervasive dimension to all existence diminishes egotism, allows individuality, softens boundaries which divide us and promotes deep community and tolerance. Conventional interpretations of power (what I'll be calling "social" power) are most closely associated with individualism and with groups competing for control. Acceptance and awareness of a depth dimension are associated with what I'll be calling "spiritual" power.

Normally, living primarily in our conventional worlds, we think of "power" as being operative in relationships in which one party seeks to control or dominate another by threatening or applying sanctions. Numerous examples are available at the level of individuals or groups. When motivated by our egos and unaware of the deep dimension of our beings, we seek to preserve and perpetuate our conditioned identities. This leads to sometimes trying to control others so that they conform to our expectations. A parent threatens punishment if a child doesn't obey. A childhood bully ridicules a playmate to enhance his self-image. A teenager makes derogatory comments about another for the same reason. An employer explicitly or implicitly says "Either you follow established practices or I'll have to let you go." A spouse withholds affection because a partner doesn't measure up to expectations. If relatively mild threats are not "successful," the desire for control can lead to verbal abuse and even acts of violence.

When threatened, members of social, economic, political, and religious groups seek to preserve their existence and defend their territory and their way of life. Unfortunately, their efforts can lead to expressions of hatred and violent actions. When this happens, they are disinclined to learn more or to listen to members of other groups, preferring instead to band together and reinforce their own perspectives. At the macro level, nations compete for resources, defend their boundaries, and threaten or apply sanctions on other nations with whom they disagree. In extreme cases, wars break out during which lethal weapons are employed, leading to the deaths of millions. Under dire circumstances, sometimes leaders emerge who increase their control and power by capitalizing on the fears and ignorance of citizens, by making promises of salvation, and by mobilizing large sectors of the population to follow their lead. When dictatorships emerge, we see the manifestation of Lord Acton's maxim first expressed in a letter to Bishop Mandell Creighton in 1887: "Power tends to corrupt; and absolute power corrupts absolutely."

These examples (whether at the level of individuals, groups, or nations) involve the exercise of "social" power because they use symbols when they seek to control others. Our earliest ancestors lived in environments dominated by survival from natural forces. They banded together to survive and sometimes conflicted with other tribes competing for available natural resources. Once individuals developed the capacity to use symbols, they formulated beliefs and rituals designed to strengthen their group identity and expressed threats using symbols. Today, while still subject to the power of our natural environment (floods, tornados, earthquakes, etc.) many conflicts occur among individuals and groups because they are embedded in their symbol-laden social structures.

In contrast to "social" power, "spiritual" power is rooted in the pervasive dimension of depth underlying all of existence. It is not ego-driven; it transcends egos. It does not involve the making of threats in order to control or dominate. When in touch with spiritual power one's individuality is recognized and that of others appreciated so there is no need to try and change them. We can disagree with other ideas and actions and even argue with them, and still respect the depth of their beings. We are not opposed to the possibility of change because we know it provides an opportunity to grow.

Spiritual power is available to everyone, sometimes in unexpected circumstances. For example, millions of people have experienced times of despair, whether from loss of a loved one, loss of a job, loss of property, or some other devastating event. It may take time, but many find the strength to pull themselves together and to carry on their life's journey. They are able to do so because, knowingly or not, they draw upon a deep reservoir of spirit that enables them to comprehend their situation in a larger perspective. It's not that they receive some special dispensation from God; they uncover a deep source of inspiration they may not know they even had.

Mahatma Gandhi drew upon spiritual power when he employed nonviolent means of combatting repression and injustice. Martin Luther King Jr. followed in his footsteps when he drew upon the depths of his being to lead the nonviolent civil rights movement. He was able to find the strength to "keep on keeping on" even in the face of the conditioned racial attitudes of the time. An assassin's bullet stopped him, but his voice still reverberates in our memories and his actions continue to inspire us. He demonstrated how spiritual power can be made manifest in social action. The same can be said for any person who refuses to be defeated by a devastating or unfair natural or social power event. Their resilience is why they are so admired.

Today, would we not be well advised to tap into this source of strength and power rather than succumb to the illusion that exercising some form of social power will benefit human relationships? We can challenge one another without resorting to violence. We can learn to love those we disagree with, not by agreeing or succumbing to them, but by recognizing that our conflicts are a function of our social conditioning and that they can be transcended by opening ourselves to the deeper dimension of our being.

The distinction I'm making between "social" and "spiritual" power bears some similarity to the distinction Erich Fromm makes between <u>power of</u> =capacity and <u>power over</u> as when it equals domination:

> But what is 'power'? It is rather ironical that this word denotes two contradictory concepts: <u>power of</u> = capacity and <u>power over</u> = domination. This contradiction, however, is of a particular kind. Power = domination results from the paralysis of power = capacity. '<u>Power over' is the perversion of 'power to.'</u> The ability of man to make productive use of his powers is his potency; the inability is his impotence....Where potency is lacking, man's relatedness to the world is perverted into a desire to dominate, to exert power over others as though they were things. Domination is coupled with death, potency with life. Domination springs from impotence and in turn reinforces it, for if an individual can force somebody else to serve him, his own need to be productive is increasingly paralyzed. (*The Art of Loving* p.88.)

Our challenge today is to choose living vitally and spontaneously instead of overly attaching ourselves to symbol systems which will eventually pass away. We can be assisted by learning ways of thinking about "love" in ways that also emphasize potency rather than domination.

# 8

## LUST AND LOVE

Tabloids are replete with examples of celebrities who have "fallen in love," who are cheating on their spouses, getting a divorce, or who are unhappy in love for one reason or another. Many TV dramas and movies are much the same. Some bestsellers tell stories of budding romances in which the flames of passion eventually diminish. Advertisements recommend products designed to enhance personal appearance, the implicit or explicit message being it will increase the chances of finding a desirable mate. These examples suggest that "love" in the popular press is predominantly an intense and fleeting emotion sought after for its promises of bliss and an end to isolation and loneliness.

As we may be identified by conditioned egos, it's natural that we seek to find a mate who will be compatible with our desires, ideas, and values. When we find someone who meets our implicit or explicit criteria, we enjoy the euphoria of falling in love. Our egos are enhanced, and trouble occurs only when unseen characteristics, patterns of behavior, or negative baggage surface to challenge the relationship. When this happens, one or both partners can lose interest in "having sex," can disapprove or be critical of perceived flaws in their partners, and can succumb to boredom, all of which can lead to the temptation of finding excitement in another relationship. Other emotions can surface in a failing partnership, such as jealousy, suspicion, or fear of rejection or betrayal. In an effort to prevent things from falling apart, one person can seek to control the other or another can be submissive lest the relationship fail. Implicit or explicit threats become more common and, in extreme cases, abuse and physical violence can ensue. Couples can survive these obstacles and even grow through them, but only if they discover they share a deep dimension transcending their individual egos.

When group members have ideas and beliefs compatible with those of another group, we "love" these groups because they reinforce our identity and make us feel more secure. We metaphorically "snuggle" and sometimes join them in alliances to perpetuate our beliefs and values. Sometimes we formalize these alliances and announce them publicly in the hope of gaining converts to our way of making sense out of the world. We fall out of love with them when they take positions at variance with ours.

In these examples, the experience of love is a function of shared symbol systems. Conventional love is fragile, subject to diminishment and disappearance. When that happens to us, we feel resentment toward our former partners, often resorting to blame and retribution. In a society obsessed with interpreting love as feeling or emotion, it's easy to see why peaceful and enduring relationships are so difficult to achieve.

Relationships have a better chance of being rewarding when couples believe there is more to love than intense physical and emotional feelings. Experiencing a deeper dimension of love doesn't rule out passionate feelings. Quite the contrary. When partners tap into a deeper dimension, they find their passion is joyful and deeply fulfilling. Passion without a deeper dimension of love is pleasurable and immediately satisfying, but temporary and often insatiable; "Making love," is far more preferable to simply "having sex."

In *The Art of Loving*, Erich Fromm offers a valuable perspective on love relationships. He argues that what sets human beings apart from the rest of nature is their experience of themselves as separate beings. Feelings associated with separation also include anxiety and the desire to overcome such alienation. According to Fromm, ways of overcoming feelings of separation include conforming to conventions, losing oneself in routinized work, or temporarily being caught up in various forms of entertainment. We may also engage in intense, but transitory, orgiastic activities such as dance, drugs, or casual sex. Some people become involved in what he calls "symbiotic" relationships that are mutually beneficial and can be passionate even though one partner controls or is controlled by the other. Whether sadistic or masochistic, partners experience union or fusion with another, but at the expense of loss of integrity. Fromm maintains that only "mature love" productively helps couples experience loving union without sacrificing their individuality. Among the characteristics of mature love are actively using one's inherent powers in ways that are giving, caring, responsible, and respectful of another's integrity. When we express these qualities, making love is passionate and joyful, not just pleasurable. Love is a process, not some substance one can receive, possess or dispense.

The theologian Paul Tillich also identifies the "urge toward the reunion of the separated" as being a deep-seated drive for all humans. In *Love, Power, and Justice* he describes different types of love, including *agape* that enters from a deep dimension and identity into the whole of life, into all the qualities of life, and into all qualities of love. "One could say that in *agape* ultimate reality manifests itself and transforms life and love. *Agape* is love cutting into love." (p. 33). "*Agape* seeks the other one in his centre," and "elevates libido into the divine unity of love, power, and justice." (p.117). If Tillich were alive today, I believe he would say that, inspired by *agape*, "having sex" becomes "making love," and pleasure becomes suffused with joy.

Another writer having similar thoughts about love is Thomas Merton in *No Man Is an Island*.

> The beginning of love is the will to let those we love be perfectly themselves, the resolution not to twist them to fit our own image. If in loving them we do not love what they are, but only their potential likeness to ourselves, then we do not love them: we only love the reflection of ourselves we find in them. (See opening chapter of his book.)

Understanding and appreciating that love emanates from the deep dimension underlying all of existence can help us soften or dissolve our grasping, egoic attachments and thereby check tendencies to dislike or be suspicious of others. Acknowledging and appreciating the deep, eternal dimension of all life replaces extremism, hatred and violence with manifestations of love and compassion.

# 9

# EMPATHY, ANTIPATHY, AND COMPASSION

Examples of empathy and antipathy abound among people at the level of what we consider to be conventional reality. Individuals and groups find it easier to have empathy with those sharing their opinions and values, and may experience antipathy toward those whose perspectives are substantially different.

Empathy and antipathy are two sides of the same coin, the coin being that both are manifestations of what we experience when we are caught up in the swirl of ideas, feelings, values, and assumptions within conventional reality and when individuals and groups are unmoored from deeper reality. We may empathize with those who agree with us because we share similar conditioning which makes it easy to identify with one another and so bolsters our egos, enhances our self-image, and increases our sense of security. The situation is different when we come into contact with persons who have different conditioning. Our antipathy may be manifested by avoiding contact with them or, in their presence, when we are reluctant to bring up topics where there may be disagreement. If a topic does come up about which we disagree, we may remain silent or feel an urge to get away, to avoid further conversation rather than risk a challenge to our egos. If we do engage, we may hear words but don't really listen. It's common to react quickly by voicing our own position and a back and forth debate ensues. If passions arise leading to enmity, even hatred of the other person or group, such animosity may lead to conflict having the potential of becoming violent.

Whether sharing with those of like mind or becoming defensive toward those having different views, we are

47

expressing our socially conditioned minds. As long as we remain trapped within our egoic patterns of thought and behavior, we won't make any progress toward more peaceful living. The solution is to recognize the limitations of our points of view, thereby opening the way for potentially fruitful dialogue. When there is tension, it's important to acquire the habit of listening, really listening, to someone who has views different from ours. It's also important to resist the temptation to presume we know where they are coming from or solely to interpret their ideas from behind the screen of our own symbol systems. Always, there is the danger of unfounded projections. This doesn't mean that we refrain from voicing our own thoughts or that we avoid contact with those having different mindsets. But it does mean that we seek to be clear about what the other is saying. One way of accomplishing this is to repeat the other's argument to make sure one understands what the other has said, or respectfully ask for clarification and elaboration for the purposes of understanding before we react in a defensive manner.

Being compassionate doesn't mean that we have to agree with one another. Quite the contrary. We need differences of opinion, different expressions of values, different interpretations of particular situations. They make up the warp and woof of our complex human tapestry and contribute to the ongoing richness of human experience. Without differences, our lives would be a bland shadow of what they could be. Realizing that we're all in this together on this speck of dust can help us have compassion for one another even when we disagree.

Being compassionate is not a sign of weakness. It requires our being strong enough to suspend our own views as we listen respectfully to others. This is different from adamantly holding on to our ideas and using some form of social power in order to get our way. Tapping into that which underlies all existence allows us to appreciate that humility is a sign of strength.

It would be different if each of us could be absolutely sure we know truth with a capital T. But we can't be sure when we disregard the many mysteries embedded in each moment and do not accept and appreciate the ultimate mystery of all existence. None of us is justified in claiming to have everything figured out. Reacting impulsively as we often do fuels conflict; responding compassionately opens the way to creative and mutual solutions and to the possibility of participating in a more peaceful world.

There is nothing new in these views about compassion. In her book, *The Case for God*, Karen Armstrong argues that compassion is a key theme in many world religions. In Buddhism, for example:

> By far the best way of achieving *anatta* ("no self") was compassion, the ability to feel with the other, which required that one dethrone the self from the center of one's world and put another there. Compassion would become the central practice of the religion. (pp. 24-25)

Discussing Confucius, Armstrong asserts that he preferred not to speak about the divine because it lay beyond the competence of language and because he considered theological chatter a distraction from the real business of religion. (p.25). Everything always came back to the importance of treating others with absolute respect. It is epitomized in the Golden Rule which, he said, his disciples should practice all day and every day. (p.25)

Referring to Judaism, Armstrong writes that when the Jewish people were exiled in Babylon during the 6th century B.C., a small circle of priests reinterpreted "old symbols and stories to build an entirely new spirituality." (p.49) Among their themes was the idea of "holiness" which "had a strong ethical component because it involved absolute respect for the sacred 'otherness' of every single creature." Later, "in Rabbinic Judaism, the religion of Israel came of age, developing the same kind of compassionate ethos as the Eastern traditions." (p.80)

Today, many are suspicious and even fearful of Muslims because of the actions of some extremist factions of that religion. But Armstrong points out: "The fundamental message of the Qur'an was not a doctrine but an ethical summons to practically express compassion: it is wrong to build a private fortune and good to share your wealth fairly and create a just society where poor and vulnerable people are treated with respect." (p.99)

It's true that the Old Testament of the Bible is replete with examples of intolerance and violence but the dominant theme of the New Testament is that of love and compassion. Among the most well-known examples are Jesus's compassion for non-Jews, for those who were unpopular, and even for the Romans who were crucifying him as when he said "Forgive them for they know not what they do." (Luke 23, verse 24).

It's important to stress the emphasis given to compassion, justice, and fairness in world religions because this message is often ignored in doctrinal disputes by religious extremists. Injustices and social power reinforce one another, and the use of violence by extremist fanatics directly contradict the theme of compassion. Abstract discussions about particular beliefs and rituals do not get to the heart of spiritual messages. Acts of compassion are badly needed to counter the injustices in our culture, to minimize the destructive tendencies of social power, and to create conditions for a more peaceful world.

Given the propensity for violence in the world today, it may seem naïve to think that compassion has a chance.

Injustices abound, all of them being associated with the exercise of *social* power. But examples of compassion are not uncommon; there are millions everyday throughout the world. Many of us greet others with a smile, a nod, or say "hello" regardless of background. Acts of kindness are common and demonstrate compassion. After a natural catastrophe, many provide direct assistance or send money to support recovery efforts without regard to the backgrounds of the victims. When friends or family members suffer a loss, most of us readily show empathy and do what we can to alleviate suffering. Millions of people volunteer to do good work in their communities and thousands of nonprofit agencies contribute to well-being in our country and around the world. In all of these instances, people show their capacity for compassion and for doing what they deem right even though they may not recognize that their actions are manifestations of the depth underlying their existence. The dimension that is always there becomes activated whenever we suspend our symbol-laden systems of thought.

# PART THREE

# RELIGION AND SPIRITUALITY

One of the aims of major world religions has been to help create a more peaceful world. Their founders were inspired by an awareness of spiritual depth but subsequent generations codified systems of belief that set the stage for conflicts among religious systems having different beliefs. Christianity is no exception. In the next two essays, I highlight conflicts within Christianity over the centuries and offer redefined treatments of some of its central concepts.

# 10

## CHRISTIAN CONFLICTS AND CONCEPTS

The Old Testament of the Bible tells the story of how the original notion of God as the "I am that I am" evolved into the beliefs and rituals of Judaism. These beliefs became dogma. Jesus in the New Testament challenged their rigidity and, while not dismissing basic principles entirely, asserted the primacy of spirit over the Law. His radically inspired work spawned numerous sects during the first centuries after his death, and their concepts and ideas evolved into what became the tenets of the Catholic Church. Centuries later, Protestantism challenged Catholicism arguing that a hierarchy of religious authorities denies individuals' direct relationship to God. Subsequently, the Protestant perspective led to the formation of various sects, each erecting their own set of beliefs and rituals.

This drastically abbreviated account doesn't do justice to the rich history of Judeo-Christianity, but it illustrates how original inspirations of the depth dimension can be covered over by complex, symbol-laden systems of belief. The advocates of different sects competed with one another and sometimes resorted to violence to spread their beliefs, for instance the Crusades, religious wars between Catholics and Protestants, the persecution of heretics, the bitter disputes among various strains of Protestants, and the efforts to convert the "heathen" throughout the new world.

Today, we still see differences between believers in conservative Christian sects who want to hold on to their traditions and those who, while not denying the value of traditions, assert the primary of spirit. The diagram on the following page provides a framework for understanding relationships among central Christian concepts and themes.

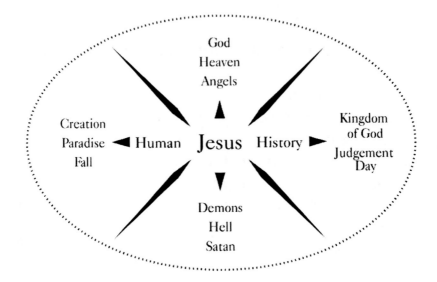

This diagram can be interpreted in different ways. Fundamentalists[6] tend to interpret it literally, considering God to be at the pinnacle of all creation and dwelling in Heaven along with angels and those souls who have accepted Jesus as their savior. Hell is the dwelling place of Satan, of the demons that plague us, and of souls who succumbed to the temptations of the devil without accepting the salvation offered by Jesus. Heaven is far above the earth and Hell is deep below with humans caught in between. Jesus merged the eternal with the temporal and suffered the crucifixion to save us from our sinful ways.

The diagram further illustrates the fundamentalist conviction that, following creation, Adam and Eve enjoyed the Garden of Eden before disobeying God's admonition not to eat forbidden fruit. They were banned (the "Fall") from paradise and were condemned to endure the challenges of human

---

[6]I distinguish between mainline fundamentalists and those who are extremist.

existence. Subsequent generations throughout history have shared this fate. When Jesus came to earth, he showed the way to salvation and to enjoying the fruits of the Kingdom of God. Those accepting Jesus as their savior will receive a favorable judgment at the end of time and will enter the heavenly Kingdom of God.

Although various sects differ in their particular interpretations of the structural elements of the diagram, billions of people over the centuries have believed in their validity and found them valuable guides to living. Numerous theologians and commentators have elaborated on them. Splendid religious architecture, music, and art illustrate their potency. Associated rituals have deep meaning for Christians everywhere who are deeply concerned about unbridled individualism, about the loss of once stable communities, about abuses of power, and about shallow expressions of love.

Some staunch believers are so convinced in the basic validity of this structured framework that they feel justified in attacking those who disagree with their interpretations. Some even resort to violence in order to preserve what they consider to be absolute truth. Just as extremist Muslims believe in creating an Islamic state, extreme Christian fundamentalists are convinced of the need to establish an earthly kingdom of God, free of non-believers who they believe deserve condemnation.

Chris Hedges, in *American Fascists: The Christian Right and the War Against America,* details the methods used by some extreme fundamentalists to win converts. He describes how they capitalize on the despair and fears of the impoverished, unemployed, and disenfranchised, and use the Bible's Book of Revelations to frighten people about a predicted final battle between Christians and nonbelievers. They promise salvation to converts who will be saved from the torture and hell that will be experienced by those who do not convert.

As long as scripture, blessed and accepted by the church, teaches that at the end of time there will be a Day of Wrath and Christians will control the shattered remnants of a world cleansed through violence and war, as long as it teaches that all nonbelievers will be tormented, destroyed and banished to hell, it will be hard to thwart the message of radical apocalyptic preachers." (p. 7)

Such a perspective appeals to some, but most conservative Christians shy away from such extremism, hatred, and violence and strive to live in accordance with their more temperate beliefs. They seem to recognize that believing in a richly structured religion is one thing; elevating those beliefs into absolutes fosters hatred and interferes with the chances of experiencing a peaceful existence.

An increasing number of Christians want to hold on to their religious beliefs, but are open to new interpretations of them. I am among those who are convinced we need not consign central concepts and themes of Christianity to the scrap heap of history. They have had, and continue to have, great value and meaning for millions. They point to the underlying wisdom embedded in the Christian tradition which can be given new life when interpreted by an awareness of the depth dimension underlying all of existence.

# 11

## REDEFINING CHRISTIAN CONCEPTS

I grew up on a farm near a small Midwestern town having two churches, one of them belonging to a Methodist denomination. My parents made sure we attended the Methodist Church every Sunday. Most pastors gave literal interpretations of the Bible. I recall questioning some of the stories they told, and I continued being skeptical of their interpretations well into adulthood. This all changed in the early 1980s when I studied Paul Tillich, Nicholai Berdyaev, Thomas Merton, and others. They showed ways of interpreting the Bible which departed from a literal understanding and analyzed central concepts metaphorically. They convinced me that Christian themes had deep meaning and resulted in my developing a great respect for Christianity in spite of its faults.

These ideas were further reinforced when I read the following writers who have commented on the movement from "religion" to "spirituality." Some focus on what they see as the decline of Protestantism. These include Robert P Jones in *The End of White Christian America,* Peter J. Leithart in *The End of Protestantism: Pursuing Unity in a Fragmented Church*, and Brian D. McClaren in *The Great Spiritual Migration: How the World's Largest Religion Is Seeking a Better Way to be Christian.* Others, such as Karen Armstrong, John Dominic Crossan, John Shelby Spong, Elaine Pagels and Marcus Borg offer interpretations of central Christian concepts which assert the primary of spirit. My studies resulted in my developing a great respect for Christianity and offering my interpretations of the following Christian themes and concepts. I became especially critical of extreme fundamentalist thinking that fosters hatred and violence.

## God

For centuries, conservative Christians have thought of God as the creator of the universe, omniscient and omnipotent, the provider of moral guidelines and the ultimate judge of who will be accepted into the Kingdom of God. This interpretation has given billions an absolute reference point as to their place in the universe, helping them to structure their lives, and helping them to make decisions when faced with challenging situations. Far right congregations have convinced themselves that God prefers them to others, justifying them to condemn, persecute, hate, and even commit violence against those who do not believe as they do. Such believers have given Christianity a bad name and led some having a secular orientation to reject and debunk Christianity entirely.

I believe in a different interpretation of God, one that doesn't question the wisdom represented by a structured belief system with God at the pinnacle. My belief challenges those who believe they are the only ones who occupy a favored place in the eyes of God. My interpretation accepts our human finiteness and considers God to be ineffable and invisible and the source of everything that exists. We cannot "know" God. We cannot fathom God. God surpasses all understanding. Ironically, only by acknowledging the limits of being human can we be aware of the deep mystery of God, God as ultimate mystery.

Although we cannot "know" God, I believe we can be aware of God. How can that be? I believe God is not only the source of the many manifestations of existence but also is immanent within all things including humans. When we become aware of this ever-present dimension, we can access the freedom, power, love, and compassion that emanates from God. In the light of God's transcendence and immanence, we can see the limitations and finiteness of our human perspectives and be inspired in ways that will influence others to see the distinction between existence and underlying spirit. Our actions can contribute to the possibility of living in a more peaceful world.

Jesus

I remember an image of a bearded, white-robed Jesus sitting in a garden greeting little children. It was located behind the pulpit of a Methodist church where preachers often described him as the Son of God who befriended strangers, who performed miracles, who inspired his followers, and who the pastor believed sacrificially endured crucifixion to save us from the stain of the Original Sin committed by Adam and Eve. This benevolent portrait conveys many of the central qualities of Jesus, but is in stark contrast to one recounted by a former colleague of mine when he visited a mega-church in Houston, Texas several years ago.

> There was a large screen at the front of the auditorium (sanctuary) which seated 16,000. The church was filled. Before the regular worship service began, patriotic songs were sung as well as religious hymns. On the screen was an image of the American flag and Jesus leading Marines into battle as jets flew overhead. The thousands seemed to be enthralled and the auditorium was filled with shouting and clapping.

A radically different view of Jesus offers an alternative perspective informed by the latest scholarly research focusing on the first few centuries after his crucifixion. (e.g. Elaine Pagels and Marcus Borg). This research suggests that Jesus was the supreme example of a person who lived a spirit-filled life, a man who, thoroughly immersed in the conditions of his time, creatively and courageously challenged his contemporaries to

61

escape the prison of their conventional thinking and to see things in a new light. He was a man who lived each day at the "cross" point of the eternal and the temporal, bringing into the world wisdom and insights that renewed and transformed those willing to listen. His message upset the dominant forces of his day and he paid the price for his courageous actions.

I believe Jesus doesn't need to be idolized as God. His words and deeds speak for themselves and are sufficient to shake up conventional mind-sets and to inspire a greater awareness of an eternal presence and of the mystery within all things. Jesus can "come alive" again, not as a resurrected spirit but as an inspirational model of what it means to live freely, creatively, and courageously. Inspired by his example, one can seek to live **as** Jesus did, sufficiently open to the divine mystery in order to meet the challenges and circumstances of our daily lives.

## Spirit

Within the richly structured system of Christian beliefs, "Spirit" often is interpreted as being dispensed from above, descending to literally inspire us in our daily lives. Jesus' disciples were so inspired and were motivated to become apostles and to spread the good news to Judea and beyond. Extreme fundamentalists sometimes adopt this theme and believe they have been chosen to be evangelists and are entitled to do the work of God and to exclude those who disagree with them.

If we consider God to be the mysterious, underlying source of all existence, then Spirit is that potency we can tap into when we see the limitations of confining patterns of thought and open ourselves to accept and not judge others. When we are so "inspired," we can give expression to spiritual power, to joyful love, to compassion, and experience the freedom of deep community with others.

This way of thinking about spirit is encouraged by influential thinkers like Paul Tillich, Nikolai Berdyaev, Thomas Merton, and many others. Tillich, in *The Eternal Now* speaks of "the holy" that is the manifestation of the presence of the ultimate. A longer passage asserts:

> The use of the term "Holy Ghost" produces an impression of great remoteness from our way of speaking and thinking. But spiritual experience is a reality for everyone, as actual as the experience of being loved or the breathing of air. Therefore, we should not shy away from the word "Spirit." We should become fully aware of the Spiritual Presence, around us and in us, even though we realize how limited our experience of "God present to our spirit" may be. (p.84)

Tillich maintains that spirit gives us joy in the midst of ordinary routine and strength in the depth of sorrow. His interpretation of "spirit" is compatible with the notion of God as "ultimate mystery," with understanding Jesus as a man challenging conventional authorities, and with interpreting power, love, and compassion as emanating from the foundation underlying all existence and available to everyone.

Heaven and Hell

During medieval times, the earth was considered the center of the universe with heaven located far above and hell deep beneath the surface. Heaven was the dwelling place of God and souls who had been "saved." Hell was the home of Satan and of souls suffering because of the way they lived their lives. Copernicus, Galileo, Kepler, Newton, and others shattered this hierarchical view of the universe yet it's not uncommon still for us sometimes to think of heaven and hell as real locations. We do so when we give thanks to God above and fear the demons that tempt us from below.

Instead of thinking of heaven as a distant location, it is better to interpret it as that state of being we experience when aware of God as ultimate mystery. We are "in heaven" when we let go of stereotypes or limited perceptions and experience deeper levels of ourselves and others. We "go to heaven" when awed by the magnificence of a cloud formation never to be duplicated or by any of the other marvels of nature. We are "in" heaven when we enjoy laughter with friends, when we respect the integrity of others, when we cease to be controlling, and when we experience joy more than superficial pleasures.

We can think of "hell" as that state of being in any moment when old mental baggage takes over and crowds out positive thoughts. We are "in hell" when we can't seem to rid ourselves of negative thoughts, when we are prisoners of self-destructive thinking. At such times, we are out of touch with the deeper spirit of our lives, making it difficult to be loving and compassionate.

When "heaven" and "hell" are conceived as temporally and spatially distant (heaven above and hell below the earth) they can be powerfully motivating, but it's relatively easy to disregard or ignore them when in the midst of daily challenges and circumstances. When they are conceived as latent within each moment, they serve as immediate reference points and inspire us to maximize the former and minimize the latter.

Sin and Salvation

When I was a child, I recall being told that a black spot will appear on my heart every time I commit a sin or break God's commandments. I could only be saved and go to heaven if I accepted Jesus into my life  Although I doubt that few now believe literally in such black spots, it's not uncommon for us to speak of those who are pure in heart and for many to believe that Jesus died to save us from our sins. Extreme fundamentalists accentuate these notions about sin and salvation when, while acknowledging their sins and accepting Jesus, presume themselves to be chosen by God to identify the sins of others and to save the world by ridding it of non-believers who are unworthy of God's grace.

My current interpretation of sin and salvation has been heavily influenced by Paul Tillich who associates sin as manifest in three interrelated kinds of separation: Separation from God, separation from others, and separation from the deeper levels of one's being. According to Tillich, when we live separate from God, we devote our life energies to building and preserving social, economic, political, religious and other created structures, reifying them rather than keeping them open and flexible. In so doing, we worship false idols, thus violating God's commandment that "you shall have no other gods before me."

When we separate from each other, we establish boundaries between ourselves and others and then treat these boundaries as real demarcations, making it easy to stereotype one another and, in turn, be stereotyped by others. Boundaries become walls, resulting in unnecessary divisions and conflicts among races, ethnic groups, classes, religious sects, political parties, or any other conventional groups. Our "sin" is treating ourselves and others as objects in the world rather than as unique persons rooted in the depth dimension underlying all of existence.

The third kind of sin is to be alienated from deeper levels of our own beings. For example, when out of touch with spirit, we are more inclined to live egocentrically than with authenticity and integrity. We are more defensive, more protective of what we perceive as our identities, and more susceptible to judging others prematurely, thus violating the commandment to love others as we love ourselves.

From Tillich's perspective, salvation is not what we may achieve at some future time by living a good life and surviving the Day of Judgment. It is what we experience at those moments, however brief, when we surrender our defenses, cease projecting our perceptions on to others, and accept the presence of divine mystery in our lives. We are "saved" when experiencing others in ways deeper than words, or when another has forgiven our transgressions. We are saved when surrendering our pride and accepting our fallibility as being only one manifestation of energy among billions of others. At such moments, we are released from the prison of our limited perspectives and can experience grace and the possibility of renewal, the kind of renewal that gives new meaning to the notion of resurrection.

Soul

Every living thing is going to die. Plants and animals decay after death and their substance mixes with the substance of other beings and form the ingredients of new life. Why should humans be any different? Is it because each of us has something called a soul which is uniquely ours, which is separate from others, and which survives after death? Within the Christian tradition, most believers would answer "yes," at least to the notion that our soul survives after the death of our bodies. For them, our souls may be accepted into heaven, descend into hell, or to some place in between. Extreme fundamentalists are convinced they are among those destined for heaven, while the souls of heathens will be condemned to hell.

The idea that we can be rejoined with our loved ones after we die has some appeal to me, but how can we be sure that will be the case? We can't KNOW. Perhaps we need to be

66

content to know that we can HAVE soul anytime we tap into a deeper dimension underlying all of existence. Perhaps we need to be content to accept that just like animals and plants, our substance will melt back into the collective totality of all existence. Ashes to ashes, dust to dust.

## The Lord's Prayer

My treatment of the foregoing concepts and themes has implications for interpreting the Lord's Prayer. Billions of people recite that prayer, individually and collectively. It's been deeply meaningful and continues to be. I suspect millions have written commentaries on its meaning, seeking to show its relevance to central concepts and themes of Christianity. I'm not at all sure how extreme fundamentalists interpret the prayer, but I offer the following as one that likely would seem foreign to their way of thinking.

Our Father,
>
> The awesome mystery present within all life, the eternal spirit breaking through to us in times of emptiness and despair,

Who art in heaven.
>
> heaven being within us rather than being some distant place, heaven being vital and creative peace,

Thy kingdom come,
>
> in all of our works today. Let our works be expressions of divine mystery in this world so that we might transform and be transformed.

Thy will be done,

> "Thy will" being not so much this work rather than that, this decision rather than that decision; instead, "Thy will" being that we manifest love in all our works and decisions.

On earth as it is in heaven,

> So that we will experience mystery within each earthly moment,

Give us this day,

> May we experience it as given, as a gift, as full of new possibilities rather than just another day.

Our daily bread,

> Bread being our challenges this day. What challenges are there for each of us to work through, to work on, to be nourished by, and to nourish?

And forgive us our trespasses,

> for, being human, we often lose touch with divine spirit and trespass on the integrity of others, not seeing them as persons with fathomless depths.

As we forgive those who trespass against us,

> For we know that others, too, are human, and are trying to make it as best they can and therefore sometimes may disregard our integrity and mystery.

And lead us not into temptation,

> into lodging our faith in idols

But deliver us from evil,
>
> From the tendencies within our beings toward isolation, distance, and separation, all of which cut us off from the light of divine mystery

For Thine is the kingdom,
>
> for which we long and which can transform our daily lives and earthly kingdoms.

The power,
>
> from which we draw our strength in times of trouble.

And the glory,
>
> which we can experience if only we accept and open our hearts to soulful spirit.

Forever and ever,
>
> beyond all notions of time, of beginning and end, of history, of temporality.

Conclusion

Heavily influenced by our conditioning, each of us has our own way of interpreting the significant concepts and themes of Christianity. May we recognize our finiteness and fallibility and resist the temptation to impose our views on others. With such recognition, we improve the chances of moving toward a more peaceful existence.

# PART FOUR

# TOWARD A MORE PEACEFUL WORLD

How would adopting a depth perspective help us move toward a more peaceful world? What would it mean to live in such a world? It doesn't mean that everything would be peaches and cream. Billions will continue to have different ideas, assumptions, beliefs, opinions. Ethnic, racial, gender, class, political, and religious differences will remain. Challenges and problems will still need to be resolved.

The difference is that people would be aware that they are not justified in thinking they are absolutely right and others are wrong. People would argue, but be tolerant of others who think differently. Compromises would replace deadlock. They would be more willing to accept their fallibility and rely upon reasoned discourse instead of reacting defensively when challenged. Realizing that each is a finite being in a complex and evolving world, people would have an underlying good will toward one another.

My final essays begin with an interpretation of an ancient Biblical theme which I believe to be profound although many dismiss it because it seems to fly in the face of what science says about human origins and evolution. They ask "Where do we go from here" and suggest that what we need is a paradigm shift, not one that formulates a new ideology, but a paradigm that is wordless, yet potent. Finally, I offer some brief thoughts on our prospects for survival.

# 12

## AN ANCIENT THEME

Many years ago, books by Karen Horney, Erich Fromm, Alan Watts, and my readings in the field of general semantics rekindled my interest in an ancient Biblical theme, the one that tells the story of Adam and Eve in the Garden of Eden. Their understanding of human development and existence struck me as analogous to the story associated with that theme. Both Christian and secular interpretations of the theme illustrate the human tendency to become so hung up by our thought structures that we foster extremism, hatred, and violence in ways that inhibit moving toward a more peaceful world.

The theme illustrates the complexity of human existence due to our ability to use symbols. Let's begin with the biblical basis of the Christian interpretation. According to the Bible, God created Adam and Eve and gave them a home in the Garden of Eden. Then,

> ... out of the ground the Lord God made to grow every tree that is pleasant to the sight and good for food, the tree of life also in the midst of the garden, and the tree of the knowledge of good and evil." (Genesis 2: 9)

God told Adam and Eve:

> You may freely eat of every tree of the garden; but of the tree of the knowledge of good and evil you shall not eat, for in the day that you eat of it you shall die. (Genesis 2: 15-17)

As the story goes, in spite of Gods warning, Adam and Eve were tempted, ate the forbidden fruit and, for the first time, knew that they were naked. They hid themselves from the presence of God and were afraid. God, knowing their disobedience, sent them from the Garden of Eden lest they eat of the tree of life and live forever. Banished from the garden, they were condemned to face the challenges of daily existence. Some interpreters of this story claim that their "original sin" is why subsequent generations have had to endure all the challenges of a worldly existence. But God did not leave his people entirely without hope. The prophet Isaiah prophesied that God will destroy the

> ...covering that is cast over all peoples, the veil that is spread over all nations. He will swallow up death forever, and the Lord God will wipe away tears from all faces, and the reproach of his people he will take away from all the earth, for the Lord has spoken. (Isaiah 25: 6-8)

This prophecy is reinforced in the New Testament by numerous passages, among them the promise that the imminent arrival of the Kingdom of God will bring an end to all human suffering.

I first heard this ancient theme as a child when listening to evangelical preachers who had been assigned to our church. They clearly believed Adam and Eve were the first humans, that there had been a Garden of Eden, and that God punished them for disobeying his command. At summer revival meetings, they preached that every person carries the scar of that original sin, that all of us are caught between yielding to the darker forces of our nature and choosing to be good, and that the only salvation for us is to accept Jesus as our savior and to obey God's commandments. The fiery depths of hell would await those who remained astray; heaven and everlasting joy would be reserved

74

for the righteous. At the end of each sermon, the preacher called for sinners to come forward to be "saved." Some members of the congregation would respond, kneeling at the altar, where the pastor would bless each one in turn.

I'm sure hundreds, if not millions, of sermons about this story have been preached over the centuries, some of them interpreting the theme literally and others doing so metaphorically. Some of the latter, perhaps without even knowing it, echoed the theme in their analysis of human existence and behavior. For example, just as Adam and Eve began their existence innocently in the Garden of Eden, so is each individual innocent in the womb and at birth. Just as Adam and Eve acquired knowledge and self-awareness, so do most children by the age of two. As Adam and Eve left the Garden of Eden to wander in the world, so does each human being leave innocence behind and experience the challenges and trials of individual existence. As the Bible promised the possibility of the Kingdom of God, so did the neo-Freudians and others believe it possible for humans to grow past their hang-ups and neuroses, and enjoy a healthy and vital existence.

After recognizing the similarities between the ancient and modern versions of this theme, I ceased dismissing it, seeing that I need not interpret it literally and that it could also be applied to the entire sweep of human history. The Garden of Eden could symbolize a time before humankind had any conscious, reflective awareness of being different from their surroundings. Adam and Eve's eating of the tree of the knowledge of good and evil could symbolize the acquisition of language leading to naming things, making distinctions, and generating knowledge. Just as they knew they were naked and covered themselves with fig leaves, so did early humans become self-aware and begin to think of themselves as separate beings. As Adam and Eve became afraid, so did our distant ancestors experience the existential anxiety of separation, leading them to construct diverse and carefully constructed symbol systems and cultural walls to alleviate their fears. As for the Kingdom of God, it could symbolize every person's hope for more peace and harmony in their individual lives and humankind's desire for a world free of war.

I'm not comfortable with either a literal or a secular interpretation of the ancient Biblical theme. The literal interpretation, albeit profound, is too simple and belies what anthropologists and historians tell us about the origins and subsequent development of multiple and divergent cultures. The secular interpretation is more palatable because it doesn't emphasize human sinfulness and is more credible because it acknowledges the positive and negative role of symbols in human development. Yet, there is something unsatisfying or unconvincing about this interpretation It comes across as very abstract and naively optimistic. It glosses over the darker side of human nature so clearly acknowledged by a strictly literal interpretation. It is also a secular interpretation through and through with no indication there might be a mysterious dimension to life that transcends intellectual formulations.

Both the literal and secular interpretations strike me as too linear. Both postulate an early state of innocence followed by a long period of conflict, but hold open the possibility of a future state of peace. Why not think of innocence, negative inclinations, and the Kingdom of God as different dimensions of our total beings? All three are present in any given moment. Sometimes, innocence and naivete' come to the surface. More often than is desirable, we display behaviors that divide and distance us from one another; but then there are special moments when we feel integrated and whole in what we do or say because we've allowed ourselves to connect with the deeper source of our beings.

This interpretation draws inspiration from many teachings in the New Testament. Jesus knew well the complex nature of the human condition. He valued innocence, experienced temptation, **and** showed what it is like to live a life inspired by God. Although several passages in the New Testament speak of a future Kingdom of God, a few others suggest that the "kingdom" is eternally immanent within us. For example, a passage from the gospel of Luke (Luke 17:20-21) quotes Jesus as asserting "The kingdom of God is not coming with signs to be observed; nor will they say, 'Lo, here it is!' or "there!' for, behold, the kingdom of God is in the midst of you." This passage suggests that the kingdom of God transcends human categories of time and space; it is eternally in the midst of us and awareness of it provides inexhaustible resources to cope with difficult times and with darker impulses and evils at large.

Yet, it isn't easy to allow the surfacing of spirit. It requires being innocent as a child, as innocent as Adam and Eve once were in the Garden of Eden. It doesn't mean that we have to refrain from efforts to know the world or that we should deny our human passions. But Jesus does caution us not to be blinded by knowledge or consumed by passions, and not to lodge faith in false idols. He encourages letting go enough to become aware of divine spirit.

I suspect that all humans can identify with one or more versions of the ancient theme. When we recall the innocence of our childhood, when we are consumed with the ideas in our heads, when we look for salvation somewhere and sometime in the future, then the language of strictly literal interpretations seems entirely appropriate. When we lose our original innocence, become burdened with old baggage, but then recognize the limitations of our individual perspectives, we can act in ways compatible with the secular interpretation. When we approach new situations aware of the depth beneath all existence, we are empowered to do so with an open mind, to use language creatively, to have compassion for the perspectives of others, thus giving expression to a spiritual interpretation of the ancient theme.

Whatever interpretation one might choose, whatever symbolic forms we use to express our "innocence," our "fall," our experience of the "kingdom," we can appreciate the profundity of the ancient Biblical theme and recognize its relevance to human existence today.

# 13

## WHERE DO WE GO FROM HERE?

Marvelous architecture, scientific discoveries, hundreds of languages, multiple cultures, great literature, technologies, religions, ideologies, inspiring music, ingenious inventions, but also extremism, hatred, violence, racism, wars, genocide, power, lust, pride, egotism, neuroses; all of these expressions and more would not constitute the stuff of human existence were it not for symbols created, used, and communicated by humans over thousands of years. Individuals and groups continue to create and use symbols to express their ideas, opinions, beliefs and values and to behave in ways to sustain and perpetuate their ways of life which can sometimes include employing violence.

So, where do we go from here? What kind of world will we leave our descendants? Will our species even survive? The answers are far from clear. What if climate change intensifies and technological advances have not met the growing energy demands of a burgeoning world population? When the world's natural resources are further diminished at the same time that destructive weapons proliferate, isn't it plausible that individuals and groups may intensify their efforts to survive, thereby giving rise to even more extremism, hatred, and violence than exist today? That doesn't have to happen, but many current trends don't hold much promise for creating a more peaceful world.

Already, we're seeing some danger signals: Increase in the number of terrorist acts, massacres here and abroad, the ongoing explicit or implicit threats of violence among nations, the actual exercise of violence among individuals and groups, cyberwarfare, the intensifying rhetoric between the far right and far left of the political spectrum. Extremist views on the right favor "Making America Great Again" by returning us to what they believe were the more placid years of earlier generations. Extremists on the left are just as adamant that we need to continue implementing progressive policies. Unfortunately, the major media outlets are not inclined to promote rational discourse about these possibilities. They seem captivated by the rhetoric on all sides and to prefer coverage which garners high ratings and financial support from advertising. Consequently, on political talk shows, representatives from either extreme sometimes seem almost gleeful as they criticize or attack the positions of their perceived opposition. The different perspectives are real and deserve rigorous discussion, but neither side seems willing to listen, really listen, to the arguments of those on the other side. They generate more noise than light and show little interest in respectfully asking probing questions which might increase understanding and foster compromise or synthesized solutions. More often than not, the same is true across the country when individuals or groups congregate to talk politics or religion.

We must find a way to short-circuit business as usual. No new religion or ideology will be the answer. Human history tells the story of the emergence of different symbol systems, their rise to dominance, and then their dissolution and replacement by another. Why should we expect that some new formulation would fare any better? What we need is a new perspective that challenges the assumptions of the one that has been in operation for centuries. The underlying assumption of that conventional paradigm has been that we humans are capable of KNOWING what is right and wrong with absolute certainty and just have to find the correct combination of symbols. Bewitched by their ability to create and use symbols, individuals and groups have competed with one another over who has the truth. It's as though all humans have been playing elaborate language games inside a huge bubble. The way forward is to burst that bubble of supposed certainty, but the problem is that very few of us are aware of the bubble, let alone wanting to give up our assumptions. Perhaps it will take a major catastrophe (disastrous climate change, ecological disaster, nuclear war, impact of an asteroid) prompting us to surrender the centuries-old perspective and to ask "What have we done?" "What are we doing?" "What can be done?" The answers we give to these questions and the choices and decisions we make will have major consequences for the kind of future we'll be leaving our descendants. Let's face it. The universe may not care one way or another what we do. But our children and grandchildren care, for it is they who will have to deal with whatever conditions we create.

A "new" paradigm is wordless. It is the indefinable dimension of depth which is the mysterious source of everything in existence. That dimension is eternal, transcending human categories of space and time. It can be pointed to, but has no structure because it cannot be described by any set of symbols. It is not really "new" for it's been the starting point for the great religions of the world when pointing out human fallibility and finitude.

Every generation faces multiple and complex issues having no easy answers. Ours is no exception, and the possibility of extinction makes them especially momentous. But the future need not be dire. Most interactions among individuals and groups are free of stress. Numerous acts of kindness occur every day. Volunteers contribute their time and energy to promote good causes. Nonprofit organizations are meeting the needs of many people. In spite of disagreements, people sometimes recognize a deeper source that transcends their differences and, when they do, they experience and exhibit an underlying sense of good will. And then there is the fact that more and more people practice meditation, making them open to accepting a mysterious deep dimension that is the source of all existence.

Accentuating these positive signs can open the way for diminishing our egoic outlooks, for growing past extremism, hatred, and violence, for manifesting spiritual power, for experiencing joyful love and deep community, and for evolving toward a more peaceful world.

Chris Hedges, in *Empire of Illusion: The End of Literacy and the Triumph of Spectacle* offers a devastating critique of our contemporary world, but then closes his book with the following assertion:

....Hope exists. It will always exist. It will not come through structures or institutions, nor will it come through nation-states, but it will prevail, even if we as distinct individuals and civilizations vanish. The power of love is greater than the power of death. It cannot be controlled. It is about sacrifice for the other—something nearly every parent understands—rather than exploitation. It is about honoring the sacred. And power elites have for millennia tried and failed to crush the force of love. Blind and dumb, indifferent to the siren calls of celebrity, unable to bow before illusions, defying the lust for power, love constantly rises up to remind a wayward society of what is real and what is illusion. Love will endure, even if it appears darkness has swallowed us all, to triumph over the wreckage that remains. (p.193)

## AUTHOR NOTE

Many thousands of years ago, visitors from outer space would have found our planet spinning and orbiting the sun with unbelievable precision. They would have found towering mountains, cascading waterfalls, spectacular cloud formations never to be duplicated, ever-changing weather systems, rivers rushing to the sea, oceans teeming with life forms and crashing onto gleaming beaches and rocky shores, flowers, magnificent redwoods, waving fields of grass, autumn foliage, cottonwood trees, stately pines, elephants, butterflies, buzzing bees, tigers, leopards, peacocks, giraffes, and so much more. They would have found millions of species changing, interacting, living, evolving, dying only to give way to new forms of life. If these same visitors were to see our planet today, they would find a new species having evolved, one which has created a dense layer of physical and mental structures made possible by the ability to use symbols, and one which seems bent on destroying itself in spite of having the ability to manifest joy and compassion.

We are so fortunate to be living on this marvelous planet. What a tragedy if we destroy our earthly home by marring it and by continuing to think hatred and violence constitute the path to peace? Let's learn to listen and have compassion for one another and for ourselves. Let's surrender foolish pride and our obsessive need to be right. Let's appreciate that we are part of nature and learn to cooperate with her. Let's accept that we are but one of millions of other species on our paradise of a planet and that our ways of seeing are so very limited. As Allen Wheelis, in The End of the Modern Age put it:

We have lived a delusion, we cannot know the world. Aided or unaided we stumble through an endless night, locked in a range of experience the limits of which are given by what we are and where we live. Earthworm or dolphin, reaching our level of investigative competence, would find a different universe; and we ourselves, in the spiral galaxy of Andromeda, would write different laws. Our eyes have seen the glory, but only within a narrow range, while by us, through us, flow vision for other eyes, music we shall never hear. We are a flicker of joy and grief and need, and shall not see the shores of this dark ocean. May we see but well enough to lay aside the weapons with which we are about to destroy, along with that little we do see, a potential of experience we know not of. (p. 115)

# APPENDIX A

# SOME RECOMMENDATIONS

## For Individuals

Recognize you are not a completely separate person.
Be willing to question your deepest assumptions, attitudes, and perceptions.
Listen, really listen, to others having different ideas.
Have compassion for yourself and toward others, including those with whom you disagree.
Practice kindness.
When with others, put away your phone and enjoy experiencing them directly.
Forgive others and yourself for transgressions.
Find time for reflection and quiet moments.
Try meditation and/or silent contemplation.
Check to see if your perceptions are accurate.
Want what you need instead of needing what you want.
Value curiosity as a means of widening your world.
Realize that you don't know all of who you are.
If you question the ideas of others, do so with the aim of understanding rather than reacting defensively.
Nurture your talents.
Practice honesty with yourself and others.
Release old emotional and mental baggage.
Appreciate that you are a unique and ongoing manifestation of spirit.
Do the best you can, with whoever you are, wherever you are.

## For Intimate Relationships

Make sure your perceptions of your partner are accurate.

Share your perceptions and invite your partner to do the same.

Realize there is no way you can be sure you are absolutely right.

Replace "having sex" with "making love."

Appreciate the depth and complexity of your mate.

Suspend judgmental attitudes.

Relinquish any desire to control your loved one.

Keep spontaneity alive.

Avoid interpretations coming only out of your projections.

Respond with empathy instead of reacting defensively.

Let each other be.

## For Groups

Become knowledgeable, in detail, of your group's history.

Be willing to accept the negatives in your group's history.

Listen to the criticisms made by other groups.

Promote non-violence.

Establish a climate for productive dialogue.

Identify and communicate goals and objectives.

# APPENDIX B

# SUPPORTIVE NOTES AND QUOTES

William Barrett, *Irrational Man:    A Study in Existential Philosophy.*

"We are so used to the fact that we forget it or fail to perceive that the man of the present day lives on a level of abstraction altogether beyond the man of the past. . .Every step forward in mechanical technique is a step in the direction of abstraction.  This capacity for living easily and familiarly at an extraordinary level of abstraction is the source of modern man's power. With it he has transformed the planet, annihilated space, and trebled the world's population.  But it is also a power which has, like everything human, its negative side, in the desolating sense of rootlessness, vacuity, and the lack of concrete feeling that assails modern man in his moments of real anxiety"  (pp 26-27)

"...we need to know what in our fundamental way of thinking needs to be changed so that the frantic will to power will not appear as the only meaning we can give to human life."  (p. 182)

"It is notorious that brilliant people are often the most dense about their own human blind spot, precisely because their intelligence, so clever in other things, conceals it from them; multiply this situation a thousand-fold, and you have a brilliant scientific and technological civilization that could run amuck out of its own sheer uprooted cleverness."  (p. 248)

Jacob Bronowski, *The Identity of Man*

"We are...mistaken if we think of our picture of the world as a passive record....The Picture is not the look of the world but our way of looking at it:  not how the world strikes us but how we construct it.  Other people and other ages had different pictures from ours, and that is why incidentally they drew differently." (p.34)

"There is no God's eye view of nature, in relativity or in any science:  only a man's eye view." (p. 37)

"We get a false picture of the world if we regard it as a set of events that have their own absolute sequence and that we merely watch....Nature is a network of happenings that do not unroll like a red carpet into time, but are intertwined between every part of the world; and we are among those parts."  (p. 37)

Martin Buber, *Between Man and Man*

"Collectivity is not a binding but a bundling together:  individuals packed together, armed and equipped in common, with only as much life from man to man as will inflame the marching step.  But community, growing community...is the being no longer side by side but with one another of a multitude of persons. "  (p. 31)

Trigant Burrow, *Prescription for Peace: The Biological Basis of Man's Ideological Conflicts" in Explorations in Altruistic Love and Behavior, ed.. By Pitirim A. Sorokin.*

"It would seem, then, that with the increase of symbol usage, something very radical biologically took place among us as a species. Our feeling-medium of contact with the environment and with one another was transferred to a segment of the organism—the symbolic segment, or forebrain." (p.111)

"With the increase of symbol usage and the coincident transfer of the organism's total motivation to this linguistic system, man developed a self-reflective type of consciousness. Interest and attention became deflected from the functional relationship of organism and environment and, to a large extent, centered on the appearance, or image, of the self and its behavior. (p. ?)

Ernst Cassirer, *An Essay on Man*

". . . . The boundaries between the kingdoms of plants, of animals, of man--the differences between species, families, genera - are fundamental and ineffaceable. But the primitive mind ignores and rejects them all. Its view of life is a synthetic, not an analytical one. Life is not divided into classes and sub-classes. It is felt as an unbroken continuous whole which does not admit of any clean-cut and trenchant distinctions. The limits between the different spheres are not insurmountable barriers; they are fluent and fluctuating. There is no specific difference between the various realms of life. Nothing has a definite, invariable, static shape." (p.81)

"By learning to name things a child does not simply add a list of artificial signs to his previous knowledge of ready-made empirical objects. He learns rather to form the concepts of those objects, to come to terms with the objective world. Henceforth the child stands on firmer ground. His vague, uncertain, fluctuating perceptions and his dim feelings begin to assume a new shape. They may be said to crystallize around the name as a fixed center, a focus of thought." (p.132)

"The function of a name is always limited to emphasizing a particular aspect of a thing, and it is precisely this restriction and limitation upon which the value of the name depends. It is not the function of a name to refer exhaustively to a concrete situation, but merely to single out and dwell upon a certain aspect. The isolation of this aspect is not a negative but a positive act. For in the act of denomination we select, out of the multiplicity and diffusion of our sense data, certain fixed centers of perception." (p.134)

"Language and science are abbreviations of reality; art is an intensification of reality." (p.143)

Ernst Cassirer, *Language and Myth.*

"...All symbolism harbors the curse of mediacy; it is bound to obscure what it seeks to reveal....All that 'denotation' to which the spoken word lays claim is really nothing more than mere suggestion; a 'suggestion' which, in face of the concrete variegation and totality of actual experience, must always appear a poor and empty shell." (p. 7)

John Dewey, *Experience and Nature*

[From my notes on Chapter III of this book.]
The universe is ever-changing and we along with it. Existence is uncertain and precarious although there also are qualities of stability and order. Within this universe at any given time we experience features of primary objects that are rich in potential meanings, uses, and values and as we carry out action-undergoings within nature we create objects of imagination and reflection that too often are erroneously taken to be superior to primary experience.

S.I Hayakawa, *Symbol, Status, and Personality*

"...Human beings live in a 'semantic environment' which is the creation of their symbol systems so that even the individual who believes himself to be in direct contact with reality, and therefore free of doctrines and assumptions, thinks in terms of the symbols with which he has been taught to organize his perceptions, namely, the visual or verbal symbols, or images, which are the currency with which communication is negotiated in his culture." (pp. 131-132)

Werner Heisenberg, *The Physicist's Conception of Nature*

"When we speak of the picture of nature in the exact science of our age, we do not mean a picture of nature so much as a picture of our relationships with nature. The old division of the world into objective processes in space and time and the mind in which these processes are mirrored ... is no longer a suitable starting point for our understanding of modern science. Science, we find, is now focused on the network of relationships between man and nature, on the framework which makes us as living beings dependent parts of nature, and which we as human beings have simultaneously made the object of our thoughts and actions. Science no longer confronts nature as an objective observer but sees itself as an actor in this interplay between man and nature. The scientific method of analyzing, explaining and classifying has become conscious of its limitations, which arise out of the fact that by its intervention science alters and refashions the object of investigation. In other words, method and object can no longer be separated" (pp. 28-29)

George Lakoff, *Women, Fire, and Dangerous Things: What Categories Reveal About the Mind*

After making reference to Hilary Putnam, Lakoff asserts:

"We are not outside of reality. We are part of it, in it. What is needed is not an externalist perspective, but an internalist perspective. It is a perspective that acknowledges that we are organisms functioning as part of reality and that it is impossible for us to ever stand outside it and take the stance of an observer with perfect knowledge, an observer with a God's eye point of view. But that does not mean that knowledge is impossible. We can know reality from the inside, on the basis of our being part of it. It is not the absolute perfect knowledge of the God's eye variety, but that kind of knowledge is logically impossible anyway.   What is possible is knowledge of another kind:  knowledge from a particular point of view, knowledge which includes the awareness that it is from a particular point of view, and knowledge which grants that other points of view can be legitimate." (p. 261)

R.E. Markham, From Journal, December 20, 1982

"Continually have to keep in mind that there is an interpenetration of the divine and earthly dimensions, the essential and the existential.  To speak of either of them separately is an abstraction.  The dimensions can be distinguished but not separated!"

R.E. Markham, From Journal, January 1, 1983.

"Every object we create, whether a physical or mental form, is unique, has a history, connections with other things which exist, and a dimension of depth."

"Our capacity to use symbols is a two-edged sword:  Used properly as tools, symbols can be the means toward appreciating the infinite subtlety and complexity of an ever-changing cosmos; used improperly, our symbol-using ability can get in the way of vital living "

93

"When overly attached to our egoic perspectives, we lose awareness of the process character of life and tend to relate to others stereotypically."

"Growing older helps us begin to understand the futility of the search for glory, of struggles for power, of efforts to forestall fate."

"Taking a relativistic stance with respect to our symbols helps nourish individual uniqueness as well as to move in the direction of greater community."

"The moves we make toward individuality can become diverted into the drive to be an individual; the moves we make toward community too often take the form of a commune or collectivity rather than deep community."

Abraham Maslow, *Toward a Psychology of Being*

"Practically every serious description of the 'authentic person' extant implies that such a person, by virtue of what he has become, assumes a new relation to his society and indeed, to society in general. He not only transcends himself in various ways; he also transcends his culture. He resists enculturation. He becomes more detached from his culture and from his society. He becomes a little more a member of his species and a little less a member of his local group." (p.11)

"The most efficient way to perceive the intrinsic nature of the world is to be more receptive than active, determined as much as possible by the intrinsic organization of that which is perceived and as little as possible by the nature of the perceiver. This kind of detached, Taoist, passive, non-interfering awareness of all the simultaneously existing aspects of the concrete, has much in common with some descriptions of the aesthetic experience and of the mystic experience. The stress is the same. Do we see the real concrete world or do we see our own system of rubrics, motives, expectations and abstractions which we have projected onto the real world? Or, to put it very bluntly, do we see or are we blind?" (p. 8)

F.S.C Northrop, *The Meeting of East and West: An Inquiry Concerning Human Understanding.*

"...it should eventually be possible to achieve a society for mankind generally in which the higher standard of living of the most scientifically advanced and theoretically guided Western nations is combined with the compassion, the universal sensitivity to the beautiful, and the abiding equanimity and calm joy of the spirit which characterize the sages and many of the humblest people of the Orient." (p. 496)

Neil Postman, *Amusing Ourselves to Death: Public Discourse in the Age of Show Business.*

"Changes in the symbolic environment are like changes in the natural environment; they are both gradual and additive at first, and then, all at once, a critical mass is achieved, as the physicists say....We have reached, I believe, a critical mass in that electronic media

95

have decisively and irreversibly changed the character of our symbolic environment. We are now a culture whose information, ideas and epistemology are given form by television, not by the printed word." (pp. 27-28)

"Typography fostered the modern idea of individuality, but it destroyed the medieval sense of community and integration. Typography created prose but made poetry into an exotic and elitist form of expression. Typography made modern science possible but transformed religious sensibility into mere superstition. Typography assisted in the growth of the nation-state but thereby made patriotism into a sordid if not lethal emotion." (p. 29)

"...We are by now so thoroughly adjusted to the 'Now...this' world of news - - a world of fragments, where events stand alone, stripped of any connection to the past, or to the future, or to other events - - that all assumptions of coherence have vanished. And so, perforce, has contradiction. In the context of <u>no context</u>, so to speak, it simply disappears." (p. 110)

Steve Taylor, *Back to Sanity:  Healing the Madness of Our Minds*
"Our basic problem...is that there really is something wrong with our minds. We suffer from a basic psychological disorder that is the source of our dysfunctional behavior, both as individuals and as a species. We're all slightly mad - but because the madness is so intrinsic to us, we're not aware of it. I call this disorder 'humania' as in 'human madness.'" (p.11)

"...although the surface of our being is filled with disturbance and negativity, underneath there is a deep reservoir of stillness and wellbeing. The surface of our being is like a rough sea, sweeping us to and fro and making us feel disoriented and anxious. But if you wear diving equipment and go beneath the surface, you're suddenly in the midst of endless silence and stillness." (p.176)

### Alan Watts, *The Way of Zen*

"The doctrine of *maya* is...a doctrine of relativity. It is saying that things, facts, and events are delineated, not by nature, but by human description, and that the way in which we describe (or divide) them is relative to our varying points of view." (p. 50)

"Certainly the world of nature abounds with surfaces and lines with areas of density and vacuity, which we employ in marking out the boundaries of events and things. But...the *maya* doctrine asserts that these forms... have no 'own-being' or 'self-nature'...; they do not exist in their own right, but only in relation to one another, as a solid cannot be distinguished save in relation to a space. In this sense, the solid and the space, the sound and the silence, the existent and the nonexistent, the figure and the ground are inseparable, interdependent, or 'mutually arising,' and it is only by maya or conventional division that they may be considered apart from one another." (p 51)

"Man's identification with his idea of himself gives him a specious and precarious sense of permanence. For this idea is relatively fixed, being based upon carefully selected memories of his past, memories which have a preserved and fixed character. Social convention encourages the fixity of the idea because the very usefulness of symbols depends upon their stability. Convention therefore encourages him to associate his idea of himself with equally abstract and symbolic roles and stereotypes, since these will help him to form an idea of himself which will be definite and intelligible. But to the degree that he identifies himself with the fixed idea, he becomes aware of 'life' as something which flows past him - faster and faster as he grows older, as his idea becomes more rigid, more bolstered with memories. The more he attempts to clutch the world, the more he feels it as a process in motion." (pp. 122-123)

"Conventional knowledge is the product of abstracting from an infinitely complex, intricate, and interconnected web of phenomena. Such conventions make communication possible but we need to realize that what is being communicated is a very partial abstraction from the complex whole." (p. ?)

Alan Watts, *The Book: The Taboo Against Knowing Who You Are*

"Don't try to get rid of the ego-sensation. Take it, so long as it lasts, as a feature or play of the total process—like a cloud or wave, or like feeling warm or cold, or anything else that happens of itself. Getting rid of one's ego is the last resort of invincible egoism! It simply confirms and strengthens the reality of the feeling. But when this feeling of separateness is approached and accepted like any other sensation it evaporates like the mirage that it is!" (p.113)

## Benjamin Whorf, *Language, Thought, and Reality*

"We dissect nature along lines laid down by our native languages. The categories and types that we isolate from the world of phenomena we do not find them there because they stare every observer in the face; on the contrary, the world is presented as a kaleidoscopic flux of impressions which has to be organized by our minds—and this means largely by the linguistic systems in our minds. We cut nature up, organize it into concepts, and ascribe significances as we do, largely because we are parties to an agreement to organize it in this way—an agreement that holds throughout our speech community and is codified in the patterns of our language. The agreement is, of course, an implicit and unstated one, BUT IT'S TERMS ARE ABSOLUTELY OBLIGATORY; we cannot talk at all except by subscribing to the organization and classification of data which the agreement decrees." (pp. 213-214)

"One significant contribution to science from the linguistic point of view may be the greater development of our sense of perspective. We shall no longer be able to see a few recent dialects of the Indo-European family, and the rationalizing techniques elaborated from their patterns, as the apex of the evolution of the human mind, nor their present widespread as due to any survival from fitness or to anything but a few events of history—events that could be called fortunate only from the parochial point of view of the favored parties. They, and our own thought processes with them, can no longer be envisioned as spanning the gamut of reason and knowledge but only as one constellation in a galactic expanse." (p. 218)

# ANNOTATED BIBLIOGRAPHY

Armstrong, Karen. *The Case for God.* New York: Alfred A. Knopf, A Division of Random House, 2009.

> Excellent historical survey of different religions' conception of God. Her emphasis on compassion as being central to all was especially helpful.

William Barrett. *Irrational Man: A Study in Existential Philosophy.* Garden City: Doubleday & Company, Inc., 1958.

> Cites numerous sources to trace the evolution of thought from a medieval mindset through the modern emphasis on science and reason, to a re-emergence of human awareness of our fallibility. Insightful presentation of the roots of existentialism and its 20<sup>th</sup> century exponents. Thorough and beautifully written.

Bernstein, Richard. *Beyond Objectivism and Relativism: Science, Hermeneutics, and Praxis.* Philadelphia: University of Pennsylvania Press .

> Thorough discussion of the debate between those who believe there are objective truths and those who believe truth is a function of time and place.

Berdyaev, Nikolai. Translated by George Reavey. *Spirit and Reality.* London: Geoffrey Bles, 1939.

> Passionate description of the dangers of objectification, the human tendency to live in a world of objects created

by one's mind which then crowds out awareness of spirit.

Boorstin, Daniel J. *The Image: A Guide to Pseudo-events in America.* New York: Harper & Row, 1962.

Surveys the many ways humans live in a swirling array of images rather than being aware of what they are representing. Thoroughly convincing.

Borg, Marcus J. *Meeting Jesus Again for the First Time: The Historical Jesus and the Heart of Christian Faith.* New York: HarperCollins, 1997.

_____. *The God We Never Knew: Beyond Religion to a More Authentic Contemporary Faith.* New York: HarperCollins Publishers, 1997.

_____. *The Heart of Christianity: Rediscovering a Life of Faith.* San Francisco: HarperCollins, 1989.

Each of Borg's books reveals the shortcomings of literal interpretations of the Bible while acknowledging their significance. One of several 21st century authors seeking new interpretations of Jesus and Christianity.

Brinton, Crane. *The Shaping of Modern Thought* Englewood Cliffs, N.J.: Prentice Hall, Inc. 1963.

Helped me understand how humans emerged from a medieval mindset to one dominated by faith in science.

Bronowski, J. *The Common Sense of Science*   Cambridge: Cambridge University Press, 1953
_____, and Mazlish, Bruce *The Western Intellectual Tradition: From Leonardo to Hegel*. New York: Harper & Row, Publishers, 1960.

> Both books focus on the rise of the scientific outlook from approximately 1500 into the 19th century. Detailed discussion of major thinkers and movements during this era.

Buber, Martin. *I and Thou,* 2nd ed. New York: Charles Scribner's Sons, 1958.

> This book is famous for his distinction between our treating each other as objects, "I-It", to our appreciating the depths of our beings, "I-Thou."

Butterfield, Herbert. *The Origins of Modern Science: 1300-1800*  New York: Collier Books, 1962.

> Anyone seeking to understand the roots of scientific thinking and how it blossomed in the modern era could benefit greatly from reading this book.

Cain, Susan. *Quiet: The Power of Introverts in a World That Can't Stop Talking.* New York: Crown Publishers, 2012. First edition.

> We are living at a time when extroverts get the most attention and are valued more highly than those who are more reflective and insightful. In the process, we are

losing the benefit of those who think more deeply and see things in longer perspective.

E.H. Carr, *The Historian and His Facts*   From the George Macaulay Trevelyan lectures, University of Cambridge, 1961.

Questions the notion that historians can discover absolute facts. Their reports are interpretations of whatever evidence exists.

Cassirer, Ernst. *An Essay on Man.* New Haven: Yale University Press, 1944.

Highlights the role of symbols in structuring human perceptions and actions.

_____ *Language and Myth.* Translated by Susanne Langer: Dover Publications, Inc., 1946.

Detailed comparison of so-called "primitive" man immersed and living in immediate interactions with nature with our living in the midst of symbols and abstractions.

Crossan, John Dominic. *Jesus: A Revolutionary Biography.* New York: HarperCollins, 1994.

Joins Marcus Borg, Elaine Pagels, and others to help us have a better understanding of the historical Jesus and how he inspired his followers and can do so today.

Dewey, John. *Experience and Nature.* New York: Dover Publications, Inc., 1929.

_____. *Logic: The Theory of Inquiry.* New York: Holt, Rinehart, and Winston, 1939

_____. *The Quest for Certainty*: Gifford Lectures. New York: G.P. Putnam's Sons, 1929.

_____. *Reconstruction in Philosophy.* Boston: Beacon Press. 1948.

_____, and Bentley, Arthur F. *Knowing and the Known.* Boston: Beacon Press, 1949.

John Dewey knew he was living in the midst of economic, scientific, political and religious developments signaling the end of the modern era and the beginning of an age yet to be clearly defined. He devoted his lifetime to exploring the ramifications of these developments and the implications of evolutionary theory. He believed it was time for what he called a reconstruction in philosophy. He often contrasted his developing positions with those of traditional philosophy and with twentieth century philosophers content to focus on matters of language and logic. His many books demonstrate a respect for both traditions but argue for pragmatic ways of thinking about the entire range of human endeavors, including morality, politics, religion, education, and logic.

Eliade, Mircea. *The Sacred and the Profane: The Nature of Religion. Translated from French: W. R. Trask.* New York: Harcourt Brace Jovanovich, 1957.

Eliade introduces the notion of the sacred and the profane as two different modes of being. The earliest cultures, tribal societies, and also pre-modern societies greatly revered the sacred mode of being. Our society has lost touch with the sacred and exemplifies the profane mode of being; it has been desacralized. The book explores the differences between these two modes,

Fromm, Erich. *The Art of Loving*. New York: Harper & Row, 1956.

_____. *Beyond the Chains of Illusion: My Encounter with Marx and Freud.* New York: Pocket Books, Inc., 1952.

_____. *Escape From Freedom*. New York: Avon Books, 1941.

_____. *Man for Himself: An Inquiry into the Psychology of Ethics.* New York: Fawcett World Library, 1947.

Fromm compares "productive" with "unproductive" love, offers illuminating interpretations of Marx and Freud, argues that modern humans' fear of freedom makes them susceptible to the rise of totalitarianism, contrasts what he calls "authoritarian" ethics with "humanistic ethics, and offers a fascinating discussion of "power," at one point asserting "...faith and power are mutually exclusive..." (Fromm, MFH, 210-211.

Hayakawa, S.I. Editor. *Our Language and Our World.* New York: Harper and Brothers, 1959.

_____. *Symbol, Status, and Personality.* New York: Harcourt & Brace, 1963.

Both books argue that symbols are abstractions from reality and operate in a dimension that is just a partial representation of that to which they refer.

Hedges, Chris. *American Fascists: The Christian Right and the War on America.* New York: Free Press, 2006.

Devastating critique of the extremist elements of fundamentalism, showing how they are undermining traditional American values and endangering our future.

_____. *Empire of Illusion: The End of Literacy and the Triumph of Spectacle.* New York: Nation Books

Equally devastating critique of contemporary society. Describes the replacement of literacy with the predominance of spectacle in different realms of human behavior.

Werner Heisenberg, *The Physicist Conception of Nature.* or *Physics and Philosophy: The Revolution in Modern Science*

Argues that we cannot know nature directly, only through our conceptual screens. Our knowledge is not of nature but is knowledge of our relationship with nature.

Hesse, Hermann. *Siddhartha.* New York: New Directions, 1857.

A novel by Hermann Hesse that deals with the spiritual journey of self-discovery of a man he calls Siddhartha. Widely considered to be a biography of Gautama Buddha.

Horney, Karen. *Neurosis and Human Growth: The Struggle Toward Self-Realization.* New York: W.W. Norton & Company, Inc., 1950.

"Under inner stress...a person may...become alienated from his real self. He will then shift the major part of his energies to the task of molding himself, by a rigid system of inner dictates, into a being of absolute perfection. For nothing short of godlike perfection can fulfill his idealized image of himself and satisfy his pride in the exalted attributes which (so he feels) he has, could have, or should have." (p. 13)

Hunter, James Davison *Culture Wars: The Struggle to Control Family, Art, Education, Law, and Politics in America.* New York: Basic Books, 1991.

Using a dialogue approach, author compares liberal and fundamentalist positions on a range of contemporary issues.

Jones, Robert P. *The End of White Christian America.* New York: Simon and Schuster, 2016.

Traces the rise and diminution of traditional Christianity, especially in its more fundamentalist forms. Sees the potential for new interpretations of central concepts and themes of Christianity.

Kaufman, Gordon D. *Relativism, Knowledge and Faith.* Chicago: The University of Chicago Press, 1960.

Sketches the general sense of rootlessness in the late 1950's, some of which can be traced to the decline of absolutistic systems and their replacement by relativistic thought. The latter can lead to nihilism, cynicism, despair, irrationality, but need not necessarily do so.

Krishnamurti, J. *Think on These Things*. New York: Harper & Row, 1964.

Challenges us not to be captivated by conventional forms and the contents of normal consciousness. Invites us to become aware of a deeper dimension and of novel views inspired by Buddhist thought. Thoroughly accessible and beautifully written.

Kuhn, Thomas S. *The Structure of Scientific Revolutions*. Chicago: The University of Chicago Press, 1962.

Prevailing scientific paradigms govern research initiatives compatible with that paradigm and only become challenged when unable to explain new phenomena, e.g. the transition from medieval to Copernican views of the cosmos and 20th century challenges to Newtonian thought. When challenge happens, the potential for new paradigms emerge.

Lakoff, George. *Women, Fire, and Dangerous Things: What Categories Reveal About the Mind* Chicago: The University of Chicago Press, 1987

Cautions against thinking our categories mirror that to which they refer.

Leihart, Peter J. *The End of Protestantism: Pursuing Unity in a Fragmented Church*. Grand Rapids, MI: Brazos Press, A Division of Baker Publishing Group, 2016.

Traces what he sees as the weakening hold of traditional Christian concepts and themes. Recognizes the resulting challenges for Christian institutions.

Marsden, George M. *Fundamentalism and American Culture: The Shaping of 20<sup>th</sup> Century Evangelicanism, 1870 to 1925.* New York: Oxford University Press, 1980.

Detailed survey of how different varieties of Protestant fundamentalism emerged in the context of major cultural events during the 20<sup>th</sup> century.

Maslow, Abraham H. *Toward a Psychology of Being.* Princeton: Van Nostrand Reinhold Company, Inc., 1962.

Especially illuminating is his discussion of what is involved in being an autonomous person.

McLaren, Brian. *The Great Spiritual Migration: How the World's Largest Religion is Seeking a Better Way to be Christian*: New York: Convergent, 2016.

This title explains well what McLaren accomplishes in this book.

McLuhan, Marshall, *The Gutenberg Galaxy: The Making of Typographic Man.* Toronto: University of Toronto Press, 1962.

_____, and Fiore, Quentin. _The Medium is the Massage: An Inventory of Effects._ New York: Bantam Books, 1967.

These books describe McLuhan's view that the typographic revolution in the 15<sup>th</sup> and 16<sup>th</sup> centuries contributed to the growing emphasis on the individual and the accompanying loss of medieval community. He explores the effects of the new mediums of radio and television upon how humans experience the world. If he were alive today, one wonders what he would have to say about the effects of our growing reliance upon digital media.

Merton, Thomas. *No Man is an Island.* San Diego: Copyright by The Abby of Our Lady of Gethsemini, 1955.

_____ *New Seeds of Contemplation.* New York: New Directions Books, 1972.

_____. *Contemplative Prayer.* Garden City, New York: Doubleday & Company, Inc., 1971.

Merton was a Catholic monk heavily influenced by Eastern religious traditions which led him to transcend, but not reject, his Catholic upbringing. In these books, he compares traditional prayers of supplication to what he considers the potency of being silent when praying.

Mills, C. Wright. *The Power Elite.* New York: Oxford University Press, 1956.

_____. *White Collar: The American Middle Classes.* New York: Oxford University Press, 1953.

Mills was one of the first to voice the alarm of the growing interrelated connections of political, economic, and military elites. In *White Collar,* Mills describes how the identity of individuals in the 1950s were increasingly defined by the organizations to which they belonged.

Northrop, F. S. C. *The Logic of the Sciences and the Humanities.* New York: Meridian Books, Inc., 1947.

_____. *The Meeting of East and West: An Inquiry Concerning World Understanding.* New York: The Macmillan Company, 1959.

> As indicated by the titles, Northrup endeavored to effect a synthesis between the sciences and humanities and to show there is no necessary conflict between the ideologies of East and West.

Novak, Martin A. *Why We Help*, p. 36 of the July 2012 issue of Scientific American Magazine.

> Argues that cooperation is as critical as competition in the struggle for survival.

Pagels, Elaine. *Beyond Belief: The Secret Gospel of Thomas.* New York: Random House, 2003.

> Pagels is thoroughly knowledgeable about the many sects during the 300 years following the crucifixion of Jesus. In this book (not one of the gospels), she identifies what she believes to be actual quotations from Jesus during his lifetime.

Piaget, Jean. *Biology and Knowledge: An Essay on the Relations Between Organic Regulations and Cognitive Processes.* Chicago: The University of Chicago Press, 1971.

> Piaget's research on early childhood illustrates his contention that the formal processes we associate with

logic have their origins in biological operations and are developed during childhood with the acquisition of language and potentially culminate in the formal operations used in adulthood.

Postman, Neil. *Amusing Ourselves to Death: Public Discourse in the Age of Show Business. New York:* Penguin Books, 1986.

"What I am claiming here is not that television is entertaining but that it has made entertainment itself the natural format for the representation of all experience....The problem is not that television presents us with entertaining subject matter but that all subject matter is presented as entertaining, which is another issue altogether." (p. 87)

Riesman, David, Glazer, Nathan, and Reuel Denney. *The Lonely Crowd: A Study of the Changing American Character.* New Haven: Yale University Press, 1961.

The authors explore the relationship between changing cultural mores and changing orientations of individuals from being "inner" directed because of internalizing traditional norms, to "other" directed resulting from getting direction from others, to "autonomy" wherein individuals set their own moral compass.

Roszak. Theodore. *The Making of a Counter-Culture: Reflections on the Technocratic Society and its Youthful Opposition.* Garden City, New York: Doubleday & Company, Inc., 1969.

This book became one of the "Bibles" of the counter-culture in the 1970's. Showed the dangers of our culture becoming so obsessed with technology that we lose touch with our deeper selves.

Ruiz, Don Miguel Ruiz. *The Four Agreements: A Practical Guide to Personal Freedom.* San Rafael, CA. Amber-Allen Publishers, 1997.

> Urges the practice of listening rather than just hearing, to pause before making reactive judgments, to avoid unreflective projections when interpreting the motivations of others.

Skinner, B.F. *Science and Human Behavior.* Toronto: The Macmillan Company, 1953.

> Developed what he considered a "scientific" approach to understanding human behavior. Challenged the notion that we have an inner agent or self that is "free" to make choices and decisions. Instead, our behavioral repertoires are products of our conditioning. We can create conditions which reinforce those behaviors we associate with being free and autonomous.

Spong, John Shelby. *Eternal Life: A New Vision: Beyond Religion, Beyond Theism, Beyond Heaven and Hell.* New York: HarperOne, 2009.

> One of several books by Spong in which he challenges literal interpretations of Christian concepts and

themes and, in their place, offers "new" and transformative perspectives.

Taylor, Barbara Brown: *Learning to Walk in the Dark Because Sometimes God Shows Up at Night.* San Francisco, CA. Harper One, 2014.

Personal account of how she overcame all-consuming fears and learned how to undercut them by tapping into a spiritual dimension.

Taylor, Steve. *Back to Sanity: Healing the Madness of Our Minds* Carlsbad, CA., Hay House, 2012.

_____ *The Calm Center: Reflections and Meditations for Spiritual Awakening, Novato, CA, New World Library, 2015.*

These two books by Taylor argue that our species has become "mad" in its expression of egoic perspectives, creating a cultural condition he calls "humania." Our path to sanity involves using meditation and other means to gain access to a deeper dimension. His writing is eloquent and even poetic at times.

_____ *The Fall: The Insanity of the Ego in Human History and the Dawning of a New Era.* London: O Books, 2005.

Thoroughly researched exposition of human evolution from a time when our distant ancestors lived in close relationships to nature to later generations in which they developed egos, to our

115

current conditions under which our egos are predominant.

Tillich, Paul. *The Courage to Be.* New Haven: Yale University Press, 1952.

_____. *Love, Power, and Justice: Ontological Analysis and Ethical Implications.* New York: Oxford University Press, 1960.

> In these two books, Tillich offers interpretations of "courage," "power," "love," and "justice" as being rooted in what he calls the "Ultimate Ground of all Being." Not easy to read, but very profound.

_____. *The Shaking of the Foundations.* New York: Charles Scribner's Sons, 1948.

_____. *The Eternal Now.* New York: Charles Scribner's Sons, 1962.

_____. *The New Being.* New York: Charles Scribner's Sons, 1955.

> These three books present sermons elucidating his conceptions of God, Jesus, and Spirit. Very insightful and accessible.

_____. *Systematic Theology: Three Volumes in One.* Chicago: The University of Chicago Press: 1963.

> As implied by the title, these three volumes constitute Tillich's thorough and erudite expression of the full

sweep of his theology. He synthesizes many significant concepts and themes of Christianity. Difficult reading, but one can gain insights by dipping into those sections of most interest.

Tolle, Eckhart. *The Power of Now: A Guide to Spiritual Enlightenment.* Novado, CA, New World Library, 1999.

_____. *A New Earth: Awakening to Your Life's Purpose.* New York: Plume, 2016.

Tolle expresses his conviction that there is a deep dimension underlying all of existence and shows how awareness of this dimension can help us transcend our egos and live more peaceful and joyful lives. Although not overly optimistic, he believes we are on the verge of potentially creating what he calls a "new earth."

Watts, Alan. *Nature, Man, and Woman.* New York: Vintage Books USA, 1970.

_____*The Book: The Taboo Against Knowing Who You Are.* New York: Vintage Books, 1966.

_____*The Way of Zen.* New York: The New American Library, 1957.

These books, and others by Watts, heavily influenced many people, especially the young who were becoming increasingly critical of the "establishment" during the 1960s and who were yearning for a spiritual perspective at variance with what they considered to be the narrowness of conventional religions. He made Zen Buddhism accessible to all who read his books.

Wheelis, Allen. *End of the Modern Age*. New York: Basic Books, 1971.

Highlights developments in science from 1500 to the mid-20<sup>th</sup> century. Argues that humans cannot **know** the world with absolute objectivity. Beautifully written.

Whorf, Benjamin Lee. Edited by John B. Carroll. *Language, Thought, and Reality.* Cambridge: The M.I.T. Press, 1956

This is a very apt title because Whorf asserts that the structure of our language affects our ways of thinking and thereby our perceptions of whatever we consider to be reality. For example, he compares what he considers to be the 'verb-oriented' language of the Hopi Indians with the "noun-oriented' languages in the Western world. The Hopis tend to see the world in terms of processes whereas Western language sees the world as consisting of objects which undergo processes.

Wilber. Ken. *No Boundary: Eastern and Western Approaches to Personal Growth.* Los Angeles: Center Publications, 1979.

From the back cover of *No Boundary*: "*No Boundary* is a simple yet comprehensive guide to the types of psychologies and therapies available from Western and Eastern sources, from psychoanalysis to Zen, existentialism to tantra....Wilber presents an easy-to-grasp map of human consciousness against which the various theories are introduced and explained.

Wittgenstein, Ludwig. *Philosophical Investigations.* Oxford, England: Blackwell Press, 1953.

The later Wittgenstein points out that our languages are not clear mirrors of reality but rather structure whatever it is we consider to be reality. Fascinating quotations relevant to the arguments of this book.

CPSIA information can be obtained
at www.ICGtesting.com
Printed in the USA
FFOW05n1616031217

*IndieReader*: Markham's proposal for the eradication of hatred centers on the existence of two realities. One, our conventional notion of reality, includes everything from mountains and molecules to thoughts and religion. The other, a deeper dimension, is the 'ultimate source of all existence,' but otherwise indefinable. Acknowledgement of this deeper dimension reveals our hubris and fallibility, and allows us to connect more authentically with others. Hatred cannot thrive in a world where we understand that, regardless of our superficial differences, we're all connected by this deeper reality.

….Becoming aware of the deep dimension (or God) results in an understanding of the ways in which symbol-laden forms of communication like language separate us from a more authentic reality.

*Kirkus Review*: Markham effectively offers a path out of what he sees as social conditioning: "We must find a way to short-circuit business as usual," he writes….Plenty of substance in these pages. A wide-ranging, thought-provoking look at faith and the nature of reality.

## About the Author:

A long-time professor of interdisciplinary studies at Massachusetts College of Liberal Arts, R.E. Markham's eclectic background includes studies in political science, sociology, philosophy, general semantics, Zen Buddhism, developmental psychology, and the theologies of Paul Tillich, Nikolai Berdyaev, and Thomas Merton. Books by Marcus Borg, Karen Armstrong, Elaine Pagels, and others proposing new interpretations of Christianity have also been influential.

ISBN 978-1-60571-376

900

9 781605 713762

*W6-BNK-393*